Sue Stratford (opposite) owns and runs The Knitting Hut, a yarn and needle supplier, and she finds the yarns she stocks there and her customers a constant source of inspiration. She teaches knitting and crochet workshops as well as offering advice to customers, and loves sharing her skills with others. She always has countless knitting projects on the go. Sue lives in Milton Keynes with her husband and five children.

Val Pierce's passion for knitting began when her father taught her to knit at the age of five. Later in life she began home knitting for yarn manufacturers, and since then she has made a huge range of items, from evening dresses to teddy bears. She later began designing items of her own, and before long Val's designs were appearing regularly in national knitting and crochet magazines. She also teaches knitting, as well as a range of other needlecrafts, to both adults and children. Val lives and works in Shropshire.

Little Christmas Decorations

to knit & crochet

First published in Great Britain 2012

Search Press Limited
Wellwood, North Farm Road,
Tunbridge Wells, Kent TN2 3DR

Based on material previously published in the 20 to Make
series as 'Mini Christmas Knits' by Sue Stratford, 2011;
and 'Mini Christmas Crochet' by Val Pierce, 2011

Text copyright © Val Pierce and Sue Stratford 2012

Photographs by Debbie Patterson (knitting) and
Paul Bricknell (crochet).

Photographs and design copyright © Search Press Ltd 2012

ISBN: 978-1-84448-870-4

The Publishers and author can accept no responsibility for
any consequences arising from the information, advice or
instructions given in this publication.

Readers are permitted to reproduce any of the items in this book
for their personal use, or for the purposes of selling for charity,
free of charge and without the prior permission of the Publishers.
Any use of the items for commercial purposes is not permitted
without the prior permission of the Publishers.

Suppliers
If you have difficulty in obtaining any of the materials and
equipment mentioned in this book, then please visit the
Search Press website for details of suppliers:
www.searchpress.com

Printed in China

Acknowledgements

Sue Stratford Thank you to everyone who
helped test knit and check these knitting
patterns and those who helped in other
ways to enable me to finish on time: Lucy,
Phyl, Bekky, Claire, Janet, Babs, Elaine, Karen,
Jennie, Pippa, Alix, Andrea, Ailsa, and last
but by no means least, Mark. Also, thanks to
my family, for whom Christmas went on a
bit longer than usual!

Val Pierce Many thanks to all the people
involved in making this book possible. Thank
you Search Press for your help and guidance,
your fantastic photography and wonderful
editing skills. Special thanks go to
Cara Ackerman and DMC for supplying the
fantastic array of Petra Yarns used to create
all the crochet projects in this book. And last
but not least, thank you to my wonderful
family and friends whose patience, help,
understanding and encouragement are
never ending.

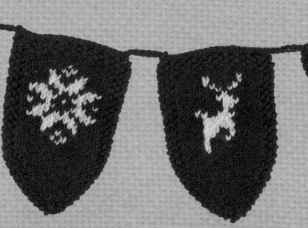

Little Christmas
Decorations
to knit & crochet

Sue Stratford
and Val Pierce

Search Press

Contents

Christmas Knits 6

Christmas Crochet 50

Christmas Knits

I have had great fun designing these quirky Christmas knits. They are quick to knit and make full use of the selection of lovely yarns out there: soft and fluffy, sparkly and shiny; all perfect for little Christmas lovelies. As themed Christmas decorations are so popular, I have knitted two versions of every pattern. One is in traditional Christmas colours (red, green and gold) and the other in a more frosty colourway, showing how easy it is to get a completely different effect by varying the yarns. The designs are all knitted using fingering (4-ply) yarn on small needles, ensuring that you get good detail. I used double-pointed knitting needles, as they are lovely and short for mini knitting, but they are not essential. Each design uses only a small amount of yarn and can be knitted quickly. However, make sure you take time when sewing them together, as a lot of the detail is achieved in the finishing.

You can use the mini knits as tree decorations, fasten them to a gift, or use them as table presents. I had a window display in my yarn shop last Christmas with a row of robins bobbing along on invisible thread, which looked fabulous. Some of the designs would make great toys.

Any tricky techniques are explained and they really help to make these little knits look extra special. Making any of these projects would be a great way to spend an evening when the nights start drawing in and Christmas is on the way.

Techniques

I-cord
To make an i-cord, cast on your stitches using a double-pointed needle, knit them and slide them to the other end of the same needle, then pull the yarn across the back of the needle and knit the stitches again. Repeat these instructions until the cord is long enough. By pulling the yarn behind the stitches on the needle, you close the 'gap' and give the appearance of French knitting. Alternatively, you can work the stitches in stocking stitch and sew up the seam.

Mattress stitch
This is a really neat way to join two pieces of stocking stitch together. The seam is practically invisible and not at all bulky. Begin by laying the work side by side with the right side facing you. Thread a darning needle with yarn and slip your needle through the horizontal bar between the first and second stitch of the first row on one piece and then repeat this process on the opposite piece. Work back and forth up this line of stitches for about 1in (2.5cm). Gently pull the yarn in the direction of the seam (upwards) and you will see the two sets of stitches join together. Repeat this process until you reach the top of the seam.

Wrap and turn
This technique ensures you do not end up with a 'hole' in your knitting when working short row shaping and turning your work mid row. Slip the following stitch from the left needle to the right needle. Move the yarn from the back to the front of the work, between the needles, and slip the stitch back to the left-hand needle. Turn the work.

Moss stitch
Row 1: (K1, P1) to end of row.
Row 2: (P1, K1) to end of row.
Therefore, on the second row you are purling the stitches you have knitted on Row 1 and knitting the stitches you have purled on Row 1.

French knots
Bring the needle up from the back of the work through to the front and wind the yarn around the needle twice. Take the needle through the work, half a stitch away, holding the loops around the needle with your finger while pulling the yarn through to the back of your work. Fasten off.

Blanket stitch
Thread a darning needle with yarn and bring to the front of your work about $^3/_8$in (1cm) from the edge. Leaving a small gap along the edge of the work, take the needle to the back of the work approximately $^3/_8$in (1cm) in from the edge and bring it back to the front at the edge of the knitting. Loop your yarn under the needle and pull it through until it lays neatly against the emerging yarn. Repeat this process.

Making up
All the mini knits are sewn together using a darning needle and the same yarn the item has been knitted in. If any other needles (e.g. a sewing needle) are required, they are shown on the individual patterns.

Abbreviations

alt:	alternate		rem:	remaining
cm:	centimetres		rep:	repeat
dec:	decrease		RS:	right side
foll:	following		skpo:	slip 1, knit 1, pass slipped stitch over
GS:	garter stitch		sl:	slip a stitch
inc:	increase		SM:	slip marker from left to right needle
K:	knit		SS:	stocking stitch
Kfb:	knit into the front and back of the stitch (increasing one stitch)		ssk:	slip 2 sts knitwise one at a time, pass the two slipped sts back to left needle, knit both together through the back of the loop
K2tog:	knit 2 stitches together			
M:	marker		ssp:	slip 2 sts knitwise one at a time, pass two slipped sts back to left needle, purl two slipped sts together from the back, left to right
M1:	make a backwards loop on your needle by twisting the yarn towards you and slipping the resulting loop on to the right-hand needle. On the following row knit or purl through the back of the st.			
			st(s):	stitch(es)
			tbl:	through the back of the loop
P:	purl		tog:	together
PM:	place marker		W&T:	wrap and turn (see opposite)
P2tog:	purl 2 stitches together		WS:	wrong side
psso:	pass slipped stitch over		YO:	yarn over needle, resulting in another stitch

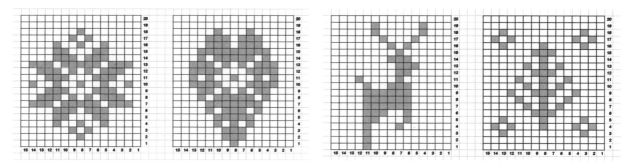

The charts for the motifs for the Nordic Bunting on pages 48–49.

Twinkling Star

Instructions:

Star points (make five)

Holding a strand of gold yarn and a strand of sequin yarn together, cast on 2 sts and K 2 rows.

Next row: K1, M1, K1 [3 sts].

K 2 rows.

Next row: K1, K1fb, K1 [4 sts].

K 1 row.

Next row: K2, M1, K2 [5 sts].

K 1 row.

Next row: K2, K1fb, K2 [6 sts].

Place sts of each point on a spare needle or stitch holder.

Centre of star

With RS facing, K across all five points of the star [30 sts].

Next row: (K1, K2tog) to end of row [20 sts].

K1 row.

Next row: K2tog to end of row [10 sts].

K1 row.

Thread yarn through rem sts and draw up, fasten off and sew side seam of star.

Make a second star shape in the same way.

Making up

With WS together, sew the stars carefully together, folding all the loose ends into the inside of the star and stuffing gently with toy filling as you go.

Starry Night

Make other stars in silver and you have a starry firmament of Christmas decorations for the tree or around the house.

Christmas Tree

Materials:

Green fingering (4-ply) yarn
Small amount of red fingering (4-ply) yarn
Red beads
Small brass bell
Toy filling
Green sewing thread and sewing needle

Needles:

1 pair 2.75mm (US 2, UK 12) knitting needles

Measurements:

Approx. 3½in (9cm) tall

Instructions:

Tree (make two)
Using green yarn, cast on 3 sts.
K 1 row.
Work inc rows as follows:
K1, M1, K to last st, M1, K1 [5 sts].
K 1 row.
Rep these 2 rows three more times [11 sts].
Cast off 3 sts at the beginning of the next 2 rows [5 sts].
Next row: K1, M1, K to last st, M1, K1 [7 sts].
K 1 row.
Rep the last 2 rows four more times [15 sts].
Cast off 4 sts at the beg of the next 2 rows [7 sts].
Next row: K1, M1, K to last st, M1, K1 [9 sts].
K 1 row.
Rep the last 2 rows five more times [19 sts].
Cast off all sts.

Trunk
Using red yarn, cast on 10 sts and work ¾in (2cm) in SS.
Cast off.

Making up
Place the two tree shapes together and sew them together, stuffing them lightly with toy filling as you go. Fold the trunk in half and attach it to the base of the tree. Sew on beads using a sewing needle and green thread. Use the picture as a guide. Attach the bell to the top of the tree.

Opposite
White Christmas
This alternative tree is made from sparkly white and silver fingering (4-ply) yarn, clear beads and a star button for a shimmering, snowy feel.

Gingerbread Heart

Materials:

Beige fingering (4-ply) yarn

Small amount of red fingering (4-ply) yarn

Red felt or a button

Spare needle/stitch holder

Toy filling

Needles:

1 pair 3.25mm (US 3, UK 10) knitting needles

Measurements:

Approx. 2¾in (7cm) from top to point of heart
(excluding hanging cord)

Instructions:

Heart shape (make two)

* Cast on 3 sts and P 1 row.

Row 2: K1, M1, K1, M1, K1 [5 sts].

Row 3: P.

Row 4: K1, M1, K2, M1, K2 [7 sts].

Cut yarn and place sts on a spare needle or st holder.

Rep instructions from * to make a second 'top' to your heart. Do not cut yarn.

Place both pieces of knitting on the same needle with WS facing.

Next row: P across both pieces [14 sts].

Work 2 rows in SS.

Next row: K2tog, K to last 2 sts, ssk [12 sts].

P 1 row.

Rep the last 2 rows a further four times until 4 sts rem.

Next row: K2tog, ssk [2 sts].

Next row: P2tog and fasten off rem st.

Making up

Place the hearts with wrong sides together and using a darning needle and beige yarn, sew the hearts neatly together, gently stuffing with toy filling as you go. Using red yarn, blanket stitch around the edges of the heart (see page 8). Attach a red felt heart or a button in the centre of the heart with a cross stitch in beige yarn. Repeat on the other side. Make a hanging cord by twisting two strands of yarn together, one beige and one red. Attach the cord to the top of the heart.

Opposite

Sparkling Heart

The alternative features shimmering white and pale blue yarn and a mother of pearl heart button in the centre.

14

Tiny Sweater

Materials:

Red fingering (4-ply) yarn
Spare needle/stitch holder

Needles:

1 pair 2.75mm (US 2, UK 12) knitting needles
Cable needle

Measurements:

Approx. 2¼in (5.5cm) tall

Abbreviations:

C4B: Place the next 2 sts on a cable needle and hold at back of work, K2, K2 sts from cable needle.

C4F: Place the next 2 sts on a cable needle and hold at front of work, K2, K2 sts from cable needle.

Instructions:

Body of sweater (make two)
Cast on 18 sts.
Work 2 rows of rib as follows:
K1, P1, to end of row.
Cable pattern:
Row 1: K.
Row 2: P.
Row 3: K5, C4B, C4F, K5.
Row 4: P.
Rep these 4 rows four more times.
Next row: Cast off 5 sts, K across the foll 8 sts and place on a st holder or spare needle, cast off rem 5 sts.

Sleeves (make two)
Cast on 8 sts and work 2 rows in K1, P1 rib.
Work 4 rows in SS.
Next row: K1, M1, K to last st, M1, K1 [10 sts].
P 1 row.
Work a further 4 rows in SS.
Cast off and fasten off yarn.

Making up
With RS facing, K across 16 held sts for the front and back of the sweater. Work in K1, P1 rib for 10 rows. Cast off in rib. Sew the shoulder seams and collar seams of the sweater. Sew the sleeves in place and sew up the sleeve and body seams. Fold over the rib neck.

Opposite
Good Wool at Christmas
These miniature sweaters make great tree decorations or comical table presents, and they don't take nearly as long to knit as the full-sized version!

Mini Mittens

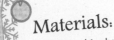

Materials:
Fingering (4-ply) self-patterning sock yarn
Toy filling

Needles:
1 pair 3.25mm (US 3, UK 10) knitting needles
Spare needle

Measurements:
Approx. $2^3/_8$in (6cm) from cuff to fingertips
with cuff folded over

Instructions:

Mitten (make two)
Cast on 20 sts and work 12 rows of K1, P1 rib.
Next row: K9, PM, K2, PM, K9. The sts between the markers will form the thumb.
P 1 row. You are now working in SS.
Next row: K to M, SM, M1, K to M, M1, SM, K to end of row [22 sts].
P 1 row.
Rep the last 2 rows until you have 8 sts between the markers [26 sts].
Next row: K9, remove marker, K across 8 sts of thumb, turn (remove 2nd marker). You will now be working just on the thumb sts.
Work 3 rows in SS.
Next row: K2tog, rep to end of row [4 sts].
Fasten off yarn.
With RS facing, rejoin yarn to the second half of the mitten and knit the 9 sts to the end of the row.
P 1 row and work across all 18 sts of mitten.

Work a further 2 rows in SS.
Next row: ssk, K5, K2tog, ssk, K5, K2tog [14 sts].
P 1 row.
Next row: ssk, K3, K2tog, ssk, K3, K2tog [10 sts].
P 1 row.
Next row: ssk, K1, K2tog, ssk, K1, K2tog [6 sts].
P 1 row.
Cast off rem sts.

Cord
To make the cord, twist a double length of yarn until it twists on itself. Alternatively, plait three lengths of yarn.

Making up
Sew the side seam of the thumb and then sew the side seam of the mitten, bearing in mind that the cuff will be folded back over the mitten and the WS of the cuff will show. Sew the cord into the tops of the mittens inside the folded cuff. Stuff a little toy filling into each mitten.

Pink Perfection

Gloves on strings take us right back to childhood winters, so these make a fun decoration or gift – perhaps for someone who always loses his or her gloves! The alternatives are knitted in soft pink and cream yarns.

Christmas Mouse

Materials:

Cream fingering (4-ply) yarn
Pale pink fingering (4-ply) yarn
2 beads for eyes
White sewing cotton
Sewing needle
Toy filling

Needles:

1 pair 3.25mm (US 3, UK 10) knitting needles,
(double-pointed needles recommended)

Measurements:

Approx. 2¾in (7cm) tall

Instructions:

Mouse body

Using cream yarn, cast on 6 sts and work 6 rows in GS.
Next row: Cast on 6, K8, (Kfb) twice, K2 [14 sts].
Next row: Cast on 6 sts and K all sts [20 sts].
Next row: K9, (Kfb) twice, K9 [22 sts].
K 2 rows.

Next row: K2tog at each end of the row [20 sts].
K 1 row.
Next row: (K2tog, K7) twice, K2tog [17 sts].
K 2 rows.
K2tog at each end of the next row, K 2 rows.
Rep from * to * until 11 sts rem.
K2tog at each end of the next row, K 1 row,
rep from * to * until 3 sts rem.
Next row: sl1, K2tog, psso, fasten off yarn.

Ears (make two)

Using cream yarn, cast on 4 sts in MC and K 1 row.
Next row: K2, M1, K2 [5 sts].
K 1 row.
Next row: K2, Kfb, K2 [6 sts].
Next row: K1, K2tog twice, K1 [4 sts].
Next row: K2tog twice [2 sts].
Next row: K2tog and fasten off yarn.

Ear linings (make two)

Cast on 3 sts using pink yarn and work 3 rows in SS.
Next row: sl1, P2tog, psso. Fasten off rem st.

Arms (make two)

Using cream yarn, cast on 4 sts and work an i-cord (see
page 8) 1in (2.5cm) long. Thread yarn through sts, pull
up tightly to gather and fasten off yarn.

Tail

Using cream yarn, cast on 4 sts and make an i-cord
approx. 2in (5cm) long.

Making up

Sew up the seam on the front of the mouse, and the nose
will automatically curl over. If the nose seems too long,
sew a thread up inside the body to the end of the nose
and then back down again, pulling as you go to shorten
the nose. Stuff with toy filling and sew up the base,
easing in as you go. Sew the ear linings to the ears and
attach the ears. Attach the arms and tail. Embroider the
nose using pink yarn. Using a sewing needle and white

sewing cotton, sew on beads for eyes and make whiskers by looping backwards and forwards through the nose. Cut the whiskers to the required length.

'Twas the Night Before Christmas…

Either of these mice would look great around your house at Christmas time, looking poised to grab any festive leftovers. The alternative is made from sparkly white yarn.

Fairy Mouse

Materials:

Pink fingering (4-ply) yarn

Small amounts of fine laceweight cream yarn and silver lurex yarn

Fine wire

Star-shaped button

Knitted Christmas Mouse (page 20)

Sewing needle

Needles:

1 pair 3.25mm (US 3, UK 10) knitting needles

Measurements:

Approx. 2¾in (7cm) tall

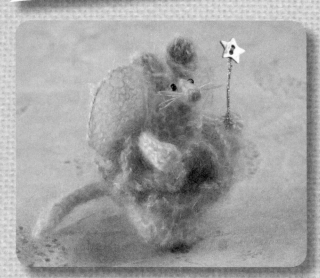

Instructions:

Tutu

Using pink yarn cast on 22 sts.

K 1 row.

Next row: Kfb into every st [44 sts].

K 1 row.

Rep these last 2 rows twice more [176 sts].

Cast off all sts.

Wings (make two)

Using fine cream yarn, cast on 3 sts.

Next row: K1, M1, K to last st, M1, K1 [5 sts].

K 1 row.

Rep the last 2 rows once more [9 sts].

K 6 rows.

Next row: K2tog, K to last 2 sts, K2tog [7 sts].

K 1 row.

Rep the last 2 rows until 3 sts rem.

Cast off.

Wand

Take a length of fine wire, fold it in half and wrap with silver lurex yarn, as shown in the picture (right). Sew the button on to the end of the wand.

Making up

Wrap the tutu twice round the mouse. Sew each end of the tutu together, securing it to the mouse. Take a length of fine wire and using the same yarn as for the wings, oversew the wire on to the edge of each wing, as shown above, leaving a length to tuck behind the tutu. Attach the wings. Sew the wand to the mouse's hand using the sewing needle.

Festive Fairies

*Turn a plain Christmas Mouse into a fairy with the addition of
a knitted tutu, wings and a tiny but very magical wand.*

Stocking

Materials:

Red fingering (4-ply) yarn

Small amount of cream and gold fingering (4-ply) yarn

Toy filling

Needles:

1 pair 3.25mm (US 3, UK 10) knitting needles

3.25mm crochet hook (optional)

Measurements:

Approx. 2½in (6.5cm) tall

Instructions:

Stocking

Using red yarn, cast on 12 sts.

Row 1 (WS): P5, PM, P2, PM, P5.

Row 2: Cast on 4 sts, K to M, M1, SM, K2, SM, M1, K to end of row [18 sts].

Row 3: Cast on 4 sts, P to M, M1, SM, P2, SM, M1, P to end of row [24 sts].

Row 4: Cast on 6 sts, K to M, M1, SM, K2, SM, M1, K to end of row [32 sts].

Row 5: Cast on 6 sts, P to M, M1, SM, P2, SM, M1, P to end of row [40 sts].

Row 6: K to M, M1, SM, K2, SM, M1, K to end of row [42 sts].

Starting with a P row, work 3 rows in SS.

Next row: K to 2 sts before M, ssk, SM, K2, SM, K2tog, K to end of row [40 sts].

Next row: P to 2 sts before M, ssp, SM, P2, SM, P2tog, P to end of row [38 sts].

Rep the last 2 rows six more times until 26 sts rem.

Remove markers and work 12 rows in SS.

Change to cream yarn and work 11 rows in GS.

Change to gold yarn and K1 row.

Cast off as follows (picot cast off):

* Cast on 2 sts, cast off 5 sts, pass st back to left-hand needle. Rep from * to the last 2 sts, cast off these sts. Fasten off yarn.

Making up

Sew the stocking's side seam, bearing in mind that the GS top will fold over so the WS will show. Sew in the ends. Attach the hook inside the stocking at the back after folding the top over. Stuff a little toy filling into the stocking.

A Very Mini Christmas!
These tiny stockings make perfect tree decorations, or you could put them out as table presents, filled with miniature gifts.

Holly Garland

Materials:

1³⁄₈in (35mm) curtain ring
Small amount of chunky yarn
Brown, green and red fingering
    (4-ply) yarn
Red beads and sewing thread
Sewing needle

Needles:

1 pair 2.75mm (US 2, UK 12) knitting needles

Measurements:

Approx 3¹⁄₈in (8cm) diameter

Instructions:

Garland
Using the brown yarn, cast on 14 sts.
* Work 4 rows in SS.
Next row (RS): K10, W&T.
Next row: P6, W&T.
Next row: K to end of row.
P 1 row.
Rep from * until the knitted strip is long enough to wrap around the curtain ring. Cast off on a K row.

Holly leaves (make nine)
Using green yarn, cast on 3 sts and work 2 rows in SS.
* Next row: Kfb three times [6 sts].
Next row: P3, M1, P3 [7 sts].
Next row: Cast off 2 sts, K to end of row [5 sts].
Next row: Cast off 2 sts, P to end of row [3 sts].
Rep from * once more.
K 1 row.
Sl1, P2tog, psso. Fasten off rem st.

Bow
Using red yarn, cast on 6 sts, working in GS until the bow measures 2¾in (7cm). Join cast on and cast off edges together. Fold flat, placing the join at the back and sew together.
Cast on 3 sts to make the tie and work ¾in (2cm) in GS. Cast off and attach to make the bow centre, pulling tightly (see picture).
Make the bow tails by casting on 4 sts and working 1in (2.5cm) in GS. Cast off and attach to the back of the bow at an angle.

Making up

To 'pad' the curtain ring, wrap with the chunky yarn. Sew the brown garland piece around the ring, joining the seam in the centre of the ring. Sew the bow on to the garland at the top of the curtain ring. Sew the holly leaves in place. Sew beads on to the holly leaves using the sewing thread and sewing needle.

Dinky Decoration

This alternative is made with pale grey and silver lurex fingering (4-ply) yarn and creates a sparkling, frosted look if you are taking a break from red and green this year.

Sweetie Cone

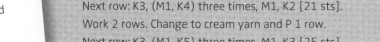

Materials:

Small amounts of cream, red, green and gold fingering (4-ply) yarn

Gold beads

Felt for lining

Sewing needle and thread

Needles:

1 pair 3.25mm (US 3, UK 10) knitting needles

Measurements:

Approx. 4in (10cm) from point to rim of cone

Instructions:

The cone is worked in SS throughout.

Using cream yarn, cast on 5 sts and work 2 rows in SS.

Next row: (K1, M1) four times, K1 [9 sts].

Work 2 rows.

Change to red yarn and P 1 row.

Next row: (K2, M1) four times, K1 [13 sts].

Work 3 rows.

Next row: K2, (M1, K3) three times, M1, K2 [17 sts].

P 1 row.

Change to gold yarn and K1 row. Change back to red yarn, P1 row.

Next row: K3, (M1, K4) three times, M1, K2 [21 sts].

Work 2 rows. Change to cream yarn and P 1 row.

Next row: K3, (M1, K5) three times, M1, K3 [25 sts].

P1 row. Change to green yarn, work 2 rows.

Next row: K3, (M1, K4) five times, M1, K2 [31 sts].

P 1 row. Change to gold yarn and K 1 row.

Change to green yarn and work 2 rows.

Change to red yarn and P 1 row.

Next row: K4 (M1, K5) five times, M1, K2 [37 sts].

P1 row.

Change to cream yarn and work 2 rows.

Change to red yarn and work 2 rows.

Cast off using a picot cast off as follows:

* Cast on 2 sts, cast off 5 sts, sl st from right-hand to left-hand needle. Rep from * until 1 st remains, cast off last st. Once you have cast off, thread the tail of the yarn through the cast off sts on the inside of the cone to pull the picot edge in and make it stand up straight, as the picot cast off will be wider than the SS cone.

Making up

Before sewing up, use the knitted cone as a pattern to cut out a piece of felt to line the cone. Carefully sew up the side of the cone using mattress stitch (see page 8), being careful to match stripes. Twist the felt lining into a cone shape and place it inside the knitted cone. Sew the top edge of the lining to the top edge of the cone to secure it. Thread approximately 9 beads on to a length of cream yarn and attach the yarn in a loop at the bottom of the cone, using the picture as a guide. Thread beads on to a length of yarn and secure each end inside the top edge of the cone to make a handle.

Sparkling Treats

This frosty looking alternative is made from pale grey, sparkly white, blue and silver lurex yarn, with silver beads. There are white and silver sweets inside for comfort on icy days.

Fir Tree Egg Cosy

Materials:

White sparkly fingering (4-ply) yarn
Small amount of silver fingering
   (4-ply) yarn
Silver beads (I used 31) and white sewing thread
Sewing needle
Toy filling

Needles:

1 pair 2.75mm (US 2, UK 12)
and 1 pair 4mm (US 6, UK 8) knitting needles

Measurements:

Approx. 3⅛in (8cm) tall

Instructions:

Egg cosy

Using a double strand of white yarn and 4mm (US 6, UK 8) knitting needles, cast on 32 sts.

Work 2 rows in GS. Starting with a P row, work 11 rows in SS.

Next row: K3, (K2tog, K4) to last 5 sts, K2tog, K3 [27 sts].

P 1 row.

K2, (K2tog, K3) to end of row [22 sts].

P 1 row.

Next row: (K1, K2tog) to last st, K1 [15 sts].

P 1 row.

Next row: K2tog to last st, K1 [8 sts].

Cut yarn, thread yarn through rem sts and use length of yarn to sew the side seam up.

Leaves

The leaves are worked in strips of triangles as follows:

Using 2.75mm (US 2, UK 12) knitting needles and MC, cast on 4 sts.

* K1 row.

K4, M1 [5 sts].

K 1 row.

K5, M1 [6 sts].

K 1 row.

K6, M1 [7 sts].

K 1 row.

K5, K2tog [6 sts].

K 1 row.

K4, K2tog [5 sts].

K 1 row.

K3, K2tog [4 sts].

These instructions make one 'point'. Repeat from * until the length of points goes around the bottom edge of the egg cosy.

Make five lengths of points: three lengths of 7 points, one of 6 points and one of 4 points. Measure as you go as you may have to adjust these numbers to fit your egg cosy.

Bobble

Using silver yarn and 2.75mm (US 2, UK 12) knitting needles, cast on 5 sts.

K 1 row.

P1, M1, P3, M1, P1 [7 sts].

Work six rows in SS.

Next row: K2tog at beginning and end of row.

Cast off rem sts.

Making up

Sew strips of leaves on to the cosy, overlapping slightly and offsetting the points on each layer. For the top section of leaves, run a length of yarn along the top edge, gather and sew on to the top of the cosy. Run a length of yarn around the edges of the bobble, fill it with a small amount of toy filling and sew it to the top of the cosy. Using a sewing needle and white thread, sew a bead on to each point, using the picture as a guide.

Rudolph

Materials:

Brown fingering (4-ply) yarn

Small amounts of cream, dark brown, black and red fingering (4-ply) yarn

³/₈in (1cm) bell

Toy filling

Needles:

1 pair 2.75mm (US 2, UK 12) knitting needles (double-pointed needles recommended)

2.75mm crochet hook (optional)

Measurements:

Approx. 3½in (9cm) nose to tail

Instructions:

Body

Using brown yarn, cast on 14 sts, P 1 row.

Work inc rows as follows:

K1, (K1fb, K1, K1fb) to last st, K1.
P 1 row [22 sts].

K1, (K1fb, K3, K1fb) to last st, K1.
P 1 row [30 sts].

K1, (K1fb, K5, K1fb) to last st, K1.
P 1 row [38 sts].

K1, (K1fb, K7, K1fb) to last st, K1.
P 1 row [46 sts].

K1, (K1fb, K9, K1fb) to last st, K1.
P 1 row [54 sts].

Work 10 rows in SS.

Work dec rows as follows:

K1, (K2tog, K9, ssk) to last st, K1.
P 1 row [46 sts].

K1, (K2tog, K7, ssk) to last st, K1.
P 1 row [38 sts].

K1, (K2tog, K5, ssk) to last st, K1.
P 1 row [30 sts].

K1, (K2tog, K3, ssk) to last st, K1.
P 1 row [22 sts].

K1, (K2tog, K1, ssk) to last st, K1.
P 1 row [14 sts].

Thread yarn through rem sts, fasten off.

Head

Using brown yarn, cast on 14 sts, P 1 row.

Work inc rows as follows:

K1, (K1fb, K1, K1fb) to last st, K1.
P 1 row [22 sts].

K1, (K1fb, K3, K1fb) to last st, K1.
P 1 row [30 sts].

Work 8 rows in SS.

Change to cream and work dec rows as follows:

K1, (K2tog, K3, ssk) to last st, K1.
P 1 row [22 sts].

K1, (K2tog, K1, ssk) to last st, K1.
P 1 row [14 sts].

Thread yarn through rem sts. Fasten off.

Bobble (nose)

Using red yarn, cast on 1 st.

Next row: knit into the front, back and front of the st [3 sts].

Starting with a K row, work 3 rows in SS.

Next row: sl1, K2tog, psso [1 st]. Run a length of yarn around the edges of the bobble, leaving a tail to attach to the head.

Antlers (make two)

Using dark brown yarn, cast on 3 sts and work an i-cord 1⁵/₈in (4cm) long (see page 8). Thread yarn through sts and fasten off. Make two more i-cords in this way, one 1in (2.5cm) long and another ⁵⁄₈in (1.5cm) long.

Legs (make four)
Using black yarn, cast on 4 sts and work 2 rows using the i-cord technique. Change to MC and continue until the leg measures 1⁵⁄₈in (4cm). Thread yarn through sts and fasten off.

Ears (make two)
Using brown yarn, cast on 3 sts, starting with a K row, work 4 rows in SS.
Next row: sl1, K2tog, psso.
Fasten off rem st.

Tail
Using brown yarn, cast on 7 sts, cast off.

Collar
Using the 2.75mm crochet hook, work a chain long enough to go around the reindeer's neck. Fasten off. Alternatively, plait a length of yarn to make the collar.

Making up
Sew the head and body seams, stuffing as you close. Attach the head to the body, using the picture as a guide. Attach the legs, tail and ears. To make the antlers, sew the shorter i-cords to the longer i-cord. Sew in the ends. Sew the antlers to the head, behind the ears. Sew the bobble to the centre of head for the nose. Using black yarn, embroider the eyes. Sew the collar in place and attach the bell.

Frosty the Red-Nosed Reindeer
This alternative reindeer is made from pale grey, blue, sparkly white and red yarn, a very magical companion to the more natural-coloured Rudolph.

Jolly Snowman

Materials:

White sparkly fingering (4-ply) yarn

Small amounts of brown, green, black and orange fingering (4-ply) yarn

Self-patterning fingering (4-ply) yarn for scarf

Toy filling

Needles:

1 pair 2.75mm (US 2, UK 12) knitting needles (double-pointed needles recommended)

Measurements:

Approx. 3¹/₈in (8cm) tall

Instructions:

Body

Using white sparkly yarn, cast on 14 sts, P 1 row.

Work increase rows as follows:

K1, (K1fb, K1, K1fb) to last st, K1. P 1 row [22 sts].

K1, (K1fb, K3, K1fb) to last st, K1. P 1 row [30 sts].

K1, (K1fb, K5, K1fb) to last st, K1. P 1 row [38 sts].

K1, (K1fb, K7, K1fb) to last st, K1. P 1 row [46 sts].

K1, (K1fb, K9, K1fb) to last st, K1. P 1 row [54 sts].

Work 2 rows in SS. Work decrease rows as follows:

K1, (K2tog, K9, ssk) to last st, K1. P1 row [46 sts].

K1, (K2tog, K7, ssk) to last st, K1. P1 row [38 sts].

K1, (K2tog, K5, ssk) to last st, K1. P1 row [30 sts].

K1, (K2tog, K3, ssk) to last st, K1. P1 row [22 sts].

K1, (K2tog, K1, ssk) to last st, K1. P1 row [14 sts].

Thread yarn through rem sts and fasten off.

Head

Using white sparkly yarn, cast on 14 sts, P 1 row.

Work inc rows as follows:

K1, (K1fb, K1, K1fb) to last st, K1. P 1 row [22 sts].

K1, (K1fb, K3, K1fb) to last st, K1. P 1 row [30 sts].

K1, (K1fb, K5, K1fb) to last st, K1. P 1 row [38 sts].

K1, (K1fb, K7, K1fb) to last st, K1. P 1 row [46 sts].

Work decrease rows as follows:

K1, (K2tog, K7, ssk) to last st, K1. P 1 row [38 sts].

K1, (K2tog, K5, ssk) to last st, K1. P 1 row [30 sts].

K1, (K2tog, K3, ssk) to last st, K1. P 1 row [22 sts].

K1, (K2tog, K1, ssk) to last st, K1. P 1 row [14 sts].

Thread yarn through rem sts and fasten off.

Nose

Using orange yarn, cast on 5 sts. P 1 row.

K2tog, K1, K2tog [3 sts].

Sl1, K2tog, psso.

Fasten off rem st.

Hat

Using green yarn, cast on 5 sts.

Next row: K1, (M1, K1) to last st, M1, K1 [9 sts].

P 1 row.

Rep the last 2 rows twice more [33 sts].

P 1 row (RS).

Starting with a P row, work 7 rows in SS.

Next row: (K2, M1) to last st, K1 [49 sts].

P 1 row.

Work 3 rows in GS. Cast off.

(Arms (make two)

Using brown yarn, cast on 4 sts and work an i-cord 1in (2.5cm) long (see page 8). Work a second i-cord just ¼in (0.5cm) long and sew it on to the first i-cord to make a 'forked' hand.

Scarf

Using self-patterning yarn, cast on 7 sts and work 4in (10cm) in GS. Cast off.

Making up

Stuff and sew the side seams of the body and head. Attach the head to the body. Sew on the arms. Sew the side seam of the hat and sew it on to the snowman's head. Sew up the nose and attach. Using French knots, embroider the eyes and buttons with black yarn and a darning needle. Tie the scarf around the snowman's neck.

White Christmas

This snowman has a cool blue look with his colour-coordinated hat and scarf set. You can use up your odds and ends of yarn dressing up these snowmen, as long as you have enough white!

Rocking Robin

Materials:
Small amounts of brown, cream, red, dark grey and orange fingering (4-ply) yarn

Toy filling

Needles:
1 pair 2.75mm (US 2, UK 12) knitting needles (double-pointed needles recommended)

Measurements:
Approx. 2³⁄₈in (6cm) diameter body

Instructions:

Body
Using cream yarn, cast on 14 sts, P 1 row.

Work inc rows as follows:

K1, (K1fb, K1, K1fb) to last st, K1. P 1 row [22 sts].

K1, (K1fb, K3, K1fb) to last st, K1. P 1 row [30 sts].

K1, (K1fb, K5, K1fb) to last st, K1. P 1 row [38 sts].

K1, (K1fb, K7, K1fb) to last st, K1. P 1 row [46 sts].

K1, (K1fb, K9, K1fb) to last st, K1. P 1 row [54 sts].

K1, (K1fb, K11, K1fb) to last st, K1. P 1 row [62 sts].

Work 2 rows in SS. Change to brown and work 4 rows in SS.

Work dec rows as follows:

K1, (K2tog, K11, ssk) to last st, K1. P 1 row [54 sts].

K1, (K2tog, K9, ssk) to last st, K1. P 1 row [46 sts].

K1, (K2tog, K7, ssk) to last st, K1. P 1 row [38 sts].

K1, (K2tog, K5, ssk) to last st, K1. P 1 row [30 sts].

K1, (K2tog, K3, ssk) to last st, K1. P 1 row [22 sts].

K1, (K2tog, K1, ssk) to last st, K1. P 1 row [14 sts].

Thread yarn through rem sts and fasten off.

Red breast
Using red yarn, cast on 14 sts and work 2 rows in SS.

Next row: K1, M1, K to last st, M1, K1. P 1 row.

Rep these 2 rows once more [18 sts].

Work 4 rows in SS.

Next row: K7, ssk, K2tog, K7 [16 sts]. P 1 row.

Rep the last 2 rows, working 2 less st before and after dec shapings until 6 sts rem.

Work 4 rows in SS.

Next row: ssk, K2, K2tog.

Cast off rem 4 sts (WS).

Beak
Using orange yarn, cast on 5 sts and P 1 row.

Next row: ssk, K1, K2tog. Thread yarn through resulting 3 sts and sew seam.

Wings (make two)
Using brown yarn, cast on 10 sts and work 2 rows in SS.

Next row: K1, M1, K to last st, M1, K1 [12 sts].

P 1 row. Rep these 2 rows once more [14 sts].

Work 2 rows in SS.

Next row: K1, ssk, K to last 3 sts, K2tog, K1 [12 sts].

P 1 row.
Rep the last 2 rows until 4 sts rem.
Next row: ssk, K2tog [3 sts].
K2tog and fasten off rem st.

Tail

Using brown yarn, cast on 7 sts and work in rib as follows:

Row 1: K1, P1 three times, K1.
Row 2: P1, K1 three times, P1.
Work a further 6 rows in K1, P1 rib.
Next row: K1, K2tog, P1, K2tog, K1 [5 sts].
Work 1 row as set in rib.
Next row: ssk, P1, K2tog [3 sts].
Work 1 row in rib and cast off rem sts.

Legs (make two)

Using dark grey yarn, cast on 4 sts and work an 'i-cord' (see page 8) 1⅝in (4cm) long. Thread yarn through sts and fasten.

Feet (make two)

Each foot consists of three 'toes'. To make each toe, cast on 4 sts using dark grey yarn and work 4 rows of 'i-cord'. Thread yarn through sts and fasten. Sew the three toes together.

Making up

Sew the side seam of the body and stuff it with toy filling without distorting the shape. Sew the breast on to the front of the body with the RS showing, using the picture as a guide. Embroider the eyes using black yarn and attach the beak. Lightly press the wings and sew them on to the body at an angle. Sew the foot to the bottom of the leg. Repeat for the second leg and sew the legs on to the body.

Frosty Friend

Robins have always featured on Christmas cards and they cheer up any winter scene. The alternative bird has a silver beak and legs with soft pink and grey feathers, and would tone in with sparkling, frosty-themed festivities.

Christmas Pud

Materials:

Small amounts of self-patterning, red, green, black and white sparkly fingering (4-ply) yarn

Stitch holder (or spare knitting needle)

Toy filling

Needles:

1 pair 2.75mm (US 2, UK 12) knitting needles

Measurements:

Approx. 2³⁄₈in (6cm) in diameter

Instructions:

Pudding

Using self-patterning yarn, cast on 14 sts, P 1 row.

Work inc rows as follows:

K1, (K1fb, K1, K1fb) to last st, K1. P 1 row [22 sts].

K1, (K1fb, K3, K1fb) to last st, K1. P 1 row [30 sts].

K1, (K1fb, K5, K1fb) to last st, K1. P 1 row [38 sts].

K1, (K1fb, K7, K1fb) to last st, K1. P 1 row [46 sts].

K1, (K1fb, K9, K1fb) to last st, K1. P 1 row [54 sts].

K1, (K1fb, K11, K1fb) to last st, K1. P 1 row [62 sts].

Work 6 rows in SS. Work dec rows as follows:

K1, (K2tog, K11, ssk) to last st, K1. P1 row [54 sts].

K1, (K2tog, K9, ssk) to last st, K1. P 1 row [46 sts].

K1, (K2tog, K7, ssk) to last st, K1. P 1 row [38 sts].

K1, (K2tog, K5, ssk) to last st, K1. P 1 row [30 sts].

K1, (K2tog, K3, ssk) to last st, K1. P 1 row [22 sts].

K1, (K2tog, K1, ssk) to last st, K1. P 1 row [14 sts].

Thread yarn through rem sts and fasten.

Small icing drips (make three)

Using white sparkly yarn, cast on 2 sts.

Work 2 rows in SS.

Cut yarn and place sts on a st holder or spare needle.

Large icing drips (make two)

Using sparkly yarn, cast on 3 sts. P 1 row.

Next row: K1, M1, K1, M1, K1 [5 sts].

P 1 row.

Cut yarn and place sts on a st holder or spare needle.

Icing top

Using white sparkly yarn, cast on as follows:

Cast on 6 sts, turn work and knit across 5 sts of large icing drip.

Turn work and cast on 6 sts, turn again and knit across 2 sts of small icing drip.

Turn work and cast on 10 sts, turn again and work across 2 sts of small icing drip.

Turn work and cast on 3 sts, turn work and knit across 5 sts of large icing drip.

Turn work and cast on 10 sts, turn work and knit across 2 sts of small icing drip. Turn work and cast on 3sts [54 sts].

P 1 row.

K1, (K2tog, K9, ssk) to last st, K1. P 1 row [46 sts].

K1, (K2tog, K7, ssk) to last st, K1. P 1 row [38 sts].

K1, (K2tog, K5, ssk) to last st, K1. P 1 row [30 sts].

K1, (K2tog, K3, ssk) to last st, K1. P 1 row [22 sts].
K1, (K2tog, K1, ssk) to last st, K1. P 1 row [14 sts].
Thread yarn through rem sts and fasten.

Holly leaves
Using green yarn, make three holly leaves following the pattern on page 26.

Making up
Sew the side seam of the pudding and stuff it with toy filling without distorting the shape. Sew the seam of the icing and sew it on top of the pudding. Sew on the holly leaves, taking care to stitch the points on the leaves evenly. Embroider French knots in red in the centre of the leaves, and in black over the pudding for raisins, using the picture as a guide.

Perfect Puds
The other pudding is made from dark brown and cream yarn and has red beads sewn on for holly berries. Both make wonderful woolly baubles for the tree.

Christmas Angel

Materials:

Blue fingering (4-ply) yarn

Small amount of cream and silver lurex fingering (4-ply) yarn

Fine laceweight cream yarn

Small amount of pink and blue embroidery thread and embroidery needle

Fine wire

Toy filling

Needles:

1 pair 2.75mm (US 2, UK 12) double-pointed knitting needles recommended)

Measurements:

Approx. 3½in (9cm) tall from top of head to bottom of dress

Instructions:

Head

Using cream yarn cast on 14 sts,

P 1 row.

Work inc rows as follows:

K1, (K1fb, K1, K1fb) to last st, K1.

P 1 row [22 sts].

K1, (K1fb, K3, K1fb) to last st, K1.

P 1 row [30 sts].

Work 4 rows in SS. Work dec rows as follows:

K1, (K2tog, K3, ssk) to last st, K1.

P 1 row [22 sts].

K1, (K2tog, K1, ssk) to last st, K1.

P 1 row [14 sts].

Thread yarn through rem sts, fasten.

Dress

Using blue yarn cast on 30 sts.

Work picot edging as follows:

K1, (cast off 2 sts, K2) five times, cast off 2 sts, K1 [18 sts].

P1 row.

Next row: K3, (M1, K4) three times, M1, K3 [22 sts].

P1 row.

Next row: K3, (M1, K4) four times, M1, K3 [27 sts].

P1 row.

Next row: K3, (M1, K4) five times, M1, K3, M1, K1 [34 sts].

P1 row.

Next row: K3, (M1, K5) five times, M1, K4, M1, K2 [41 sts].

P1 row.

Work lace edging as follows:

Next row: K2, *(K2tog) four times, (K1, YO) four times. Rep from * three times. K3.

K 3 rows.

Rep these 4 rows twice more.

Cast off.

Sleeves

Using blue yarn, cast on 20 sts.
K 2 rows.
Starting with a K row, continue in SS for 4 rows.
Next row: K1, K2tog, K to last 3 sts, ssk, K1 [18 sts].
P 1 row.
Rep the last 2 rows a further three times until you have 12 sts left.
K 2 rows. Cast off.

Wings (make two)

Using fine cream yarn, cast on 5 sts.
K 2 rows.
Next row: K1, M1, to last st, M1, K1 [7 sts].
K 1 row.
Rep these 2 rows three more times [13 sts].
K 6 rows.
Next row: K2tog, K to last 2 sts, K2tog [11 sts].
K 1 row.
Rep the last 2 rows three more times until 5 sts rem.
Cast off.

Legs (make two)

Using cream yarn, cast on 4 sts. Work an i-cord (see page 8) 3½in (9cm) long, or adjust the length so that the legs show beneath the dress.

Arms (make two)

Using cream yarn, cast on 4 sts. Work an i-cord long enough to stick out of the sleeves.

Making up

Stuff and sew up the head. Embroider French knots on to the head to make hair using silver lurex yarn. Embroider the eyes and a mouth using embroidery thread. Attach the legs to the bottom of the head. Lightly press the dress as the shape will distort slightly when you work the lace edging. Sew up the back seam of the dress and gather it at the top, then sew it to the base of the head. Sew up the sleeve seams, attaching the arms as you go. Using the laceweight yarn, oversew a length of fine wire to the edges of the wings. Tuck the wire inside the dress at the back of the angel's head and sew the wings in place. Bend a length of wire into a halo shape and wrap it in silver lurex yarn. Attach it to the angel's head.

Treetop Angel

Knit your own heavenly host, changing the colours to suit your Christmas colour scheme.

What a Hoot

Materials:
Brown chunky yarn

Small amounts of beige, brown, red, cream and gold coloured fingering (4-ply) yarn

Gold lurex fingering (4-ply) yarn

Toy filling

Small brass bell

Two buttons and matching thread

Sewing needle

Needles:
1 pair 2.75mm (US 2, UK 12) and 1 pair 4.5mm (US 7, UK 7) knitting needles

Measurements:
Approx. 4in (10cm) tall

Instructions:

Body (make two)

Using 4.5mm (US 7, UK 7) needles and chunky yarn, cast on 12 sts and work 2 rows in SS.

Next row: K1, M1, K to last st, M1, K1 [14 sts].

P 1 row.

Rep last 2 rows once more [16 sts].

Continue in SS for 10 rows.

Next row: K1, ssk, K to last 3 sts, K2tog, K1 [14 sts].

P 1 row.

Rep these 2 rows once more [12 sts].

Work 2 rows in SS.

Next row: K1, ssk, K to last 3 sts, K2tog, K1 [10 sts].

Next row: P4, cast off 2 sts, P to end of row [8 sts].

Turn and working on the first 4 sts, K1, ssk, K1 [3 sts].

P 1 row.

Next row: sl1, K2tog, psso. Fasten off rem st.

With RS facing, rejoin yarn to rem 4 sts, K1, K2tog, K1 [3 sts].

P 1 row.

Next row: sl1, K2tog, psso. Fasten off rem st.

Base

Using 4.5mm (US 7, UK 7) needles and chunky yarn, cast on 3 sts. Work 2 rows in SS.

Next row: K1, M1, K1, M1, K1 [5 sts].

P 1 row.

Rep the last 2 rows once more [7 sts].

Work 2 rows in SS.

Next row: K1, ssk, K1, K2tog, K1 [5 sts].

P 1 row.

Next row: K1, ssk, K2tog, K1 [3 sts].

P 1 row [3 sts].

Cast off rem sts.

Tummy

Using gold yarn and 2.75mm (US 2, UK 12) knitting needles, cast on 10 sts, P 1 row.

Next row: K1, M1, K to last st, M1, K1 [12 sts].

P 1 row.

Rep the last 2 rows twice more [16 sts].

Work 4 rows in SS.

Next row: K6, ssk, K2tog, K6 [14 sts].

P 1 row.

Rep the last 2 rows, working one less st before and after decreases until 6 sts rem. Cast off rem sts.

Eyes

Cast on 4 sts using beige yarn and 2.75mm (US 2, UK 12) knitting needles. P 1 row.

Next row: K1, M1, K2, M1, K1 [6 sts].

P 1 row.

Work in SS for 4 rows.

Next row: ssk, K2, K2tog [4 sts].

P 1 row. Cast off rem sts.

Beak

Cast on 5 sts using gold lurex yarn and 2.75mm (US 2, UK 12) needles and work 2 rows in SS.

Next row: K2tog, K1, K2tog.

P 1 row.

Thread yarn through rem 3 sts and sew up seam of beak.

Wings

Cast on 3 sts using brown yarn and 2.75mm (US 2, UK 12) knitting needles.

The wings are worked in GS throughout.

K 2 rows.

Next row: K1, M1, K to end of row [4 sts].

K 1 row.

Rep the last 2 rows until you have 8 sts.

Knit 12 rows.

Next row: K1, K2tog, K to last 3 sts, K2tog, K1.

K 1 row.

Rep the last 2 rows until 4 sts rem.

Next row: K2tog twice, cast off rem st and fasten off yarn.

Hat

Using 2.75mm (US 2, UK 12) needles and cream yarn, cast on 22 sts and work 12 rows in GS.

Change to red yarn.

Work 8 rows in SS.

Next row: (K1, K2tog) seven times, K1 [15 sts].

P 1 row.

Next row: (K1, K2tog) to end of row [10 sts].

P 1 row.

Work 2 rows in SS.

Next row: K2tog to end of row [5 sts].

P 1 row.

Thread yarn through rem sts, sew up side seam of hat, pulling the yarn slightly as you sew so the top of the hat folds over slightly. Fold GS edging up.

Making up

Sew up the side seams and stuff the owl with toy filling. Sew in the base, adding a piece of card to strengthen it if required. Attach the tummy, beak, wings and knitted eyes. Using a sewing needle and matching thread, sew on buttons for eyes. Attach the bell to the top of the hat.

French Hen

Materials:

Small amount of chunky yarn

Small amounts of red, orange, black and self-patterning fingering (4-ply) yarn

Two stitch holders

Toy filling

Needles:

1 pair 4.5mm (US 7, UK 7) and
1 pair 2.75mm (US 2, UK 12) knitting needles

Measurements:

Approx. 4in (10cm) tall

Instructions:

Body

Using chunky yarn and 4.5mm (US 7, UK 7) knitting needles, cast on 31 sts.

Next row: (K4, M1) seven times, K3 [38 sts].

P 1 row. Continue in SS until work measures 2³⁄₈in (6cm).

Next row: K5 and turn, placing rem sts on a holder. P 1 row.

You are now working the tail.

Next row: K3, K2tog [4 sts].

Next row: P2, P2tog [3 sts] K 1 row.

Next row: sl1, P2tog, psso. Fasten off rem st.

With WS facing, rejoin yarn to opposite end of the row, P5 and turn (second half of tail).

Next row: K2tog, K3 [4 sts].

Next row: P2tog, P2 [3 sts]. K 1 row.

Next row: sl1, K2tog, psso. Fasten off rem st.

28 sts remain. Shape head as follows:

With RS facing, slip rem 6 sts on to holder and rejoin yarn. K across next 16 sts, sl rem 6 sts on to a holder.

Next row: P7, PM, P2, PM, P7.

Next row: K2tog, K to last 2 sts, SM, K2tog. P1 row [14 sts].

Next row: K2tog, K4, M1, SM, K2, SM, M1, K4, K2tog [14 sts].

Next row: P6, M1, SM, P2, SM, M1, P6 [16 sts].

Next row: K7, M1, SM, K2, SM, M1, K7 [18 sts].

Remove markers. You will now be working on one side of the head.

Next row: P2tog, P5, P2tog, turn work leaving rem 9 sts on your needle.

** Next row: K2tog, K3, K2tog. P2tog, P1, P2tog. Cast off rem 3 sts.

With WS facing, rejoin yarn to held sts and work as follows:

P2tog, P5, P2tog. Work from ** to end.

Cast off the rem 12 sts.

Wings (make two)

Using chunky yarn and 4.5mm (US 7, UK 7) needles, cast on 5 sts, K 1 row.

Row 1: K1, M1, K to last st, M1, K1 [7 sts].

K 1 row.

Rep these 2 rows twice more [11 sts].

K 1 row.

Next row: K2tog, K to last 2 sts, K2tog [9 sts].

Next row: K to last 2 sts, K2tog [8 sts].

Cast off 2 sts, K to end [6 sts].

Next row: K2tog, K2, K2tog [4 sts].

Next row: K2tog, K to end of row [3 sts].

Base

Using chunky yarn and 4.5mm (US 7, UK 7) needles, cast on 3 sts. K1, M1, K to last st, M1, K1 [5 sts].

P 1 row.

Rep these 2 rows a further three times [11 sts].

Continue in SS until work measures 1¾in (4.5cm).

Next row: K1, K2tog, K to last 3 sts, K2tog, K1.

P 1 row.

Rep last 2 rows until 5 sts rem.

Next row: K2tog, K1, K2tog. Cast off rem 3 sts.

Beak

Using 2.75mm (US 2, UK 12) knitting needles and orange yarn, cast on 5 sts and P1 row.

K2tog, K1, K2tog [3 sts]. P 1 row.

Thread yarn through rem sts and fasten off.

Comb

Using red yarn and 2.75mm (US 2, UK 12) needles, cast on 2 sts, K 1 row.

M1, K2. K 1 row.

* Cast off 2 sts [1 st].

Next row: M1, K1. K 1 row.

Next row: M1, K2. K 1 row. Rep from * once more. Cast off.

Tail feathers (make five)

Using chunky yarn and 4.5mm (US 7, UK 7) knitting needles, cast on 6 sts, cast sts off.

Scarf

Using self-patterning yarn and 2.75mm (US 2, UK 12) knitting needles, cast on 7 sts. Work 7⁷/₈in (20cm) in GS. Cast off and sew in the ends.

Making up

Sew the seams of the body together. Stuff and sew on the base. You can cut a piece of card to fit inside the base to make it flat. Sew the seam of the beak and attach it. Sew the wings, comb and tail feathers in place using the pictures as a guide. Embroider the eyes using French knots.

Turtle Dove

Instructions:

Body

Using red yarn, cast on 10 sts and work 6 rows in SS.

Next row: K4, PM, K2, PM, K4.

P 1 row.

Next row: K to M, M1, SM, K2, SM, M1, K to end of row [12 sts].

P 1 row.

Rep the last 2 rows a further six times until 24 sts rem.

Work 2 rows in SS.

Next row: K to 2 sts before M, ssk, SM, K2, SM, K2tog, K to end of row [22 sts].

P 1 row.

Rep the last 2 rows until 18 sts rem.

Next row: K1, M1, K to 2 sts before M, ssk, SM, K2, SM, K2tog, K to last st, M1, K1 [18 sts].

Next row: P1, M1, P to 2 sts before M, ssp, SM, P2, SM, P2togtbl, P to last st, M1, P1 [18 sts].

Next row: K to 2 sts before M, ssk, SM, K2, SM, K2tog, K to end of row [16 sts].

P 1 row.

Next row: K1, ssk, K2, ssk, SM, K2, SM, K2tog, K2, K2tog, K1 [12 sts].

P 1 row.

Change to gold yarn.

Next row: K2tog, rep to end of row [6 sts].

P 1 row.

Next row: K2tog, rep to end of row [3 sts].

Thread yarn through rem sts and fasten off.

Tail feathers

Make three of each in cream and gold.

Cast on 2 sts and K 8 rows.

Next row: K1, M1, K1 [3 sts].

K 12 rows.

Next row: sl1, K2tog, psso. Fasten off rem st.

Large feathers for wings

Make four of each in cream and gold.

Cast on 2 sts and K 4 rows.

Next row: K1, M1, K1 [3 sts].

K 8 rows.

Next row: sl1, K2tog, psso. Fasten off rem st.

Small feathers for wings

Make two in gold.

Cast on 2 sts and K 4 rows.

Next row: K1, M1, K1 [3 sts].

K 5 rows.

Next row: sl1, K2tog, psso. Fasten off rem st.

Making up
Sew the seam of the bird, stuffing with toy filling as you go. Embroider a French knot on each side of the head for the eyes. Attach the tail feathers. Sew two larger feathers together and attach them to the sides of the bird. Sew the smaller feathers on top of the larger ones to shape the wings.

Nordic Bunting

Materials:
Red fingering (4-ply) yarn
Small amount of cream fingering (4-ply) yarn

Motifs:
The charts for the motifs are on page 9.

Needles:
1 pair 3.25mm (US 3, UK 10) knitting needles
3mm (US D-0, UK 11) crochet hook (optional)

Measurements:
Each pennant approx. 4¼in (11cm) high and
2¾in (7cm) wide

Instructions:
Using red yarn, cast on 1 st.
Next row: K into the front, back and front of the stitch [3 sts].
Next row: K1, P1, K1.
Next row: K1, M1, P1, M1, K1 [5 sts].
Next row: K1, P1, K1, P1, K1.
Next row: K1, P1, M1, K1, M1, P1, K1 [7 sts].
Next row (RS): K1, P1, K3, P1, K1.
Next row: (K1, P1) three times, K1.
Continue as follows:
Row 1: **K1, P1, K1**, M1, work to last 3 sts, M1, **K1, P1, K1**.
Row 2: **K1, P1, K1**, work to last 3 sts, **K1, P1, K1**.
Keeping the 3 border sts in Moss st (marked in bold), work these 2 rows a further six times, inc either side of the central SS panel until you have 21 sts.
Work 2 rows with no further shaping.
Keeping Moss st edges, work 20 rows of your selected chart (see page 9).
Work a further 2 rows.
Work 4 rows in Moss st. Cast off all sts.

Making up
Either sew the corners of the pennants together or crochet across the top of each pennant to join them together.

48

Christmas Crochet

'Christmas comes but once a year and when it does it brings good cheer', so why not bring your very own cheer to this magical time of year by creating some or all of the delightful little crocheted decorations I have designed for this book.

There is nothing quite like making your own tree hangings, either for yourself or to give as a special gift to a close friend or relative. They can be packed away and used year after year and even handed down through the generations, giving you and your family pleasure for many years to come. Some of the pieces are free-standing, but there is no reason why you shouldn't add hanging loops and use them to adorn your Christmas tree too.

My favourite colours are reds, golds and greens, but all the items can be crocheted in whatever yarns or colours you want to match your particular Christmas theme, whether it be traditional, cool and trendy, or simple and childlike.

All of the designs can be made quickly and easily using scraps and oddments of yarn, so even those new to crochet will be able to make an impressive collection of novelty knits for the festive season. Add a tiny gift inside the cracker, or use it instead of a place card at the Christmas dinner table; use sparkly yarns, beads and sequins, or even embroider on a name to make these novelty knits truly your very own creation. Whatever you decide to do I am sure that you will have as much fun making them as I did designing them.

Happy Christmas crocheting!

51

Hints and tips

American and British crochet terminology

In all the patterns, US terms are given first, followed by the UK terms afterwards in brackets. So US single crochet would be written as sc (*UKdc*) and US double crochet as dc (*UKtr*).

The most frequently used terms are:

American	British
slip stitch (sl st)	slip stitch (sl st)
chain stitch (ch)	chain stitch (ch)
single crochet (sc)	double crochet (dc)
half double crochet (hdc)	half treble crochet (htr)
double crochet (dc)	treble crochet (tr)
treble crochet (tr)	double treble crochet (dtr)
double treble crochet (dtr)	triple treble crochet (trtr)
skip	miss

Materials

All the decorations are made using a size 2.00mm (US B-1, UK 14) crochet hook, though for the Christmas Bear you will also need a 4.00mm (US G-6, UK 8) crochet hook. Either a no. 5 or no. 3 crochet cotton is used throughout, though if you prefer a fine fingering (4-ply) yarn can be used instead. Most of the items use only small amounts of yarn, making them ideal for using up scraps and oddments.

You will also need various embellishments, including bows, stars, ribbons, buttons and beads; a sewing needle and thread; craft glue; and toy stuffing.

Measurements

Approximate measurements of all the pieces are provided, but remember that if you use different yarns from those specified, the finished sizes may vary.

Techniques

Some of the decorations are worked in the round, which is sometimes a little difficult to master, so always place a marker at the beginning of the round so that you know where you started; it is very easy to end up with either too many or too few stitches if you don't know where the row began.

One or two of the designs are stuffed as you make them, and again this is a technique that you will need to get used to. It does make it a little difficult to crochet sometimes, especially when the opening is quite small. The secret is to add only tiny bits of stuffing at a time.

This magical little tree is perfect for adorning the Christmas dinner table (see pattern on page 84). Make one for every guest at your festive gathering – a wonderful little keepsake for them to take home and treasure!

Pine Cones

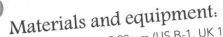

Materials and equipment:

Crochet hook size 2.00mm (US B-1, UK 14)

Gold metallic yarn – 1 ball

Holly berry embellishment

20in (0.5m) of narrow gold ribbon

Toy stuffing

Craft glue

Sewing needle and gold thread (optional)

Measurements:

The pine cone is approximately 2in (5cm) high.

Special abbreviations:

3dc (*UKtr*) cluster – draw up loop, yrh, hook into space, draw up loop, repeat 3 times, yrh, draw through all loops, 1 ch to secure.

4dc (*UKtr*) cluster – as above but repeat 4 times.

Instructions:

Using gold metallic yarn, make 6 ch then join with sl st into a ring.

Round 1: work 12 sc (*UKdc*) into the ring then join with a sl st.

Round 2: work a 3dc (*UKtr*) cluster into each sc (*UKdc*), join with a sl st to top of first 3dc (*UKtr*) cluster [12 3dc (*UKtr*) clusters].

Round 3: sl st into first space between clusters, work 3dc (*UKtr*) cluster, 1 ch into each space, join with a sl st to top of first 3dc (*UKtr*) cluster.

Round 4: sl st into next 2 ch sp, work *4dc (*UKtr*) cluster, 1 ch* into each 2 ch sp, join with a sl st to top of first 4dc (*UKtr*) cluster.

Round 5: repeat round 4.

Round 6: sl st into next 2 ch sp, *3dc (*UKtr*) cluster, 1 sc (*UKdc*)* into each 2 ch sp, join with a sl st to top of 3dc (*UKtr*) cluster.

Round 7: sl st into next 2 ch sp, 3dc (*UKtr*) cluster into each 1 ch sp, but omit the 1 ch to secure, join as previous round.

To make up

Carefully push tiny pieces of stuffing inside the pine cone using the crochet hook to help you. Do not overstuff – just get a pleasing shape.

Using a small amount of craft glue, attach the holly berry embellishment to the top of the pine cone. Thread ribbon through the last row of clusters. Decide how long you want the ribbon loop to be and trim the ribbon as necessary. Either tie the ends of the ribbon together in a knot or stitch them to form a loop.

54

Festive Wreath

Materials and equipment:

Crochet hook size 2.00mm (US B-1, UK 14)
No. 5 crochet cotton – 1 ball of dark green,
    1 ball of light green
3 small holly berry embellishments
20in (0.5m) of narrow green satin ribbon
Gold ribbon bow or a short length of gold
    ribbon to tie in a bow
Gold bell
Craft glue
Sewing needle and green thread (optional)

Measurements:

The wreath is approximately 2¾in (7cm)
in diameter.

Instructions:

Using light green crochet cotton, make 50 ch.
Row 1: Work 2 dc (*UKtr*) into 3rd ch from hook, 3 dc
(*UKtr*) into each ch to end. As you work, the crochet will
twirl into a tight corkscrew shape.
Use dark green cotton to make another twist in the
same way.

To make up
Secure both the light green and dark green crochet
twists together at one end, then twine the strips around
each other, folding the coils inside one another as you
do so, until you get a neat double coil. Join the two ends
together firmly.

Glue the holy berry embellishments on the coil at
random, tucking them inside the twists. Glue the ribbon
bow and bell at the top of the wreath to cover the join
where the ends of the twists meet.

Thread the ribbon through the top of the wreath to
make a hanging loop. Decide how long you want the
ribbon loop to be and trim the ribbon as necessary. Either
tie the ends of the ribbon together in a knot or stitch
them to form a loop.

Dove of Peace

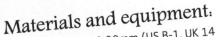

Materials and equipment:

Crochet hook size 2.00mm (US B-1, UK 14)

No. 3 crochet cotton – 1 ball of pale lilac, 1 ball of pale blue and small amounts of yellow and black

Small amount of gold metallic yarn

Gold ribbon rose

20in (0.5m) of narrow lilac ribbon

Needle and lilac thread

Small amount of stuffing

Measurements:

The dove is approximately 2¼in (6cm) high and 3½in (9cm) long.

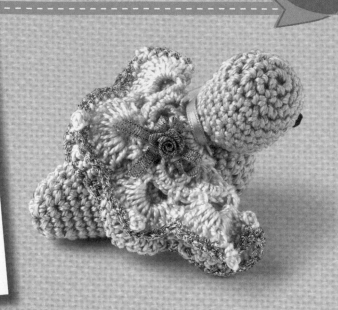

Instructions:

Head

Using lilac crochet cotton, make 2 ch.

Round 1: work 6 sc (*UKdc*) into 2nd ch from hook then join with a sl st to form a tight circle.

Round 2: 2 sc (*UKdc*) into each st around [12 sts].

Round 3: *1 sc (*UKdc*) into next sc (*UKdc*), 2 sc (*UKdc*) into next sc (*UKdc*),* repeat from * to * all around [18 sts].

Round 4: *1 sc (*UKdc*) into each of next 2 sc (*UKdc*), 2 sc (*UKdc*) into next sc (*UKdc*),* repeat from * to * all around [24 sts].

Rounds 5–9: work in sc (*UKdc*) all around.

You will now begin decreasing. Stuff the head before you close it up.

Round 10: *1 sc (*UKdc*) into each of next 2 sc (*UKdc*), sc (*UKdc*) 2 tog,* repeat from * to * all around.

Round 11: work in sc (*UKdc*) all around.

Round 12: *1 sc (*UKdc*) in next sc (*UKdc*), sc (*UKdc*) 2 tog,* repeat from * to * all around.

Round 13: work in sc (*UKdc*) all around.

Round 14: sc (*UKdc*) 2 tog all around, join with a sl st.

Fasten off.

Body

Using lilac crochet cotton, make 2 ch.

Round 1: work 6 sc (*UKdc*) into 2nd ch from hook then join with a sl st to form a tight circle.

Round 2: 2 sc (*UKdc*) into each sc (*UKdc*) around [12 sts].

Round 3: *1 sc (*UKdc*) into next sc (*UKdc*), 2 sc (*UKdc*) into next sc (*UKdc*),* repeat from * to * all around [18 sts].

Round 4: *1 sc (*UKdc*) into each of next 2 sc (*UKdc*), 2 sc (*UKdc*) into next sc (*UKdc*),* repeat from * to * all around [24 sts].

Round 5: * 1 sc (*UKdc*) into each of next 3 sc (*UKdc*), 2 sc (*UKdc*) into next sc (*UKdc*),* repeat from * to * all around [30 sts].

Rounds 6–12: work in sc (*UKdc*) all around.

You will now begin decreasing. Stuff the body before you close it up.

Round: 13: *1 sc (*UKdc*) into each of next 3 sc (*UKdc*), sc (*UKdc*) 2 tog,*

repeat from * to * all around.
Rounds 14–16: work in sc (*UKdc*)
all around.
Round 17: *1 sc (*UKdc*) into each of
next 2 sc (*UKdc*), sc (*UKdc*) 2 tog,*
repeat from * to * all around.
Rounds 18–20: work in sc (*UKdc*)
all around.
Round 21: *1 sc (*UKdc*) into next sc
(*UKdc*), sc (*UKdc*) 2 tog,* repeat from
* to * all around.
Rounds 22–23: work in sc (*UKdc*)
all around.
Round 24: sc (*UKdc*) 2 tog all around.
Rounds 25–26: work in sc (*UKdc*).
Fasten off. This is the tail end.

Wings
Using blue crochet cotton, make 8 ch
then join with a sl st into ring.
Round 1: 7 ch to count as 1 dtr
(*UKtrtr*) and 2 ch, *1 dtr (*UKtrtr*) 2 ch
into ring,* repeat from * to * 14 times
more then join with a sl st to 5th ch of
starting ch [sixteen 2 ch sp].
Round 2: 2 ch, 2 sc (*UKdc*) into first 2
ch sp, *3 sc (*UKdc*) into next 2 ch sp,*
repeat all around and join with a sl st
to beg [48 sts].
Round 3: 8 ch for first sc (*UKdc*) and
7 ch loop, 1 sc (*UKdc*) into 3rd sc
(*UKdc*), *5 ch, miss 2 sc (*UKdc*), 1 sc
(*UKdc*) into next sc (*UKdc*), 7 ch, miss
2 sc (*UKdc*), 1 sc (*UKdc*) into next sc
(*UKdc*),* repeat from * to * all around,
ending last repeat 5 ch, join with sl st
to beg.
Round 4: sl st into first 7 ch loop,
into loop work 3 ch, 4 dc (*UKtr*), 4 ch,
sl st into 3rd ch from hook (1 picot
made), 1 ch, 5 dc (*UKtr*) into loop, *1
sc (*UKdc*) into next 5 ch loop, [5dc
(*UKtr*), 4 ch, sl st into 3rd ch from
hook (1 picot made), 5 dc (*UKtr*)] all
into next 7 ch loop,* repeat from * to
* all around, join with a sl st to beg.
Fasten off.

Round 5: join in gold to any point
and work 1 row of sc (*UKdc*) all
around, join with a sl st and fasten
off.

Beak
Using yellow crochet cotton, make
7 ch. Work 1 sc (*UKdc*) into 2nd ch
from hook, 1 sc (*UKdc*) into each ch
to end. Fasten off.

To make up
Sew the head to the body at a slight
angle. Embroider the eyes on the
head, then fold the beak in half
lengthways and stitch in position
on the head. Fold the wings in half,
matching the points, then stitch
them to the centre of the back. Glue
the ribbon rose on top.

Thread the lilac ribbon through the
top of the body to make a hanging
loop. Decide how long you want the
ribbon loop to be and trim the ribbon
as necessary. Either tie the ends
of the ribbon together in a knot or
stitch them to form a loop.

Glimmering Snowflake

Instructions (make two):

Using white crochet cotton, make 8 ch then join with sl st into a ring.

Round 1: 7 ch to count as 1 dtr (*UKtrtr*) and 2 ch, *1 dtr (*UKtrtr*) 2 ch into the ring,* repeat from * to * 14 times more, then join with a sl st into 5th ch of starting ch [sixteen 2ch sp].

Round 2: 2 ch, 2 sc (*UKdc*) into first 2ch sp, *3 sc (*UKdc*) into next 2ch sp,* repeat all around and join with a sl st to beg [48 sts].

Round 3: 8 ch, for first sc (*UKdc*) and 7 ch loop, 1 sc (*UKdc*) into 3rd sc (*UKdc*), *5 ch, miss 2 sc (*UKdc*), 1 sc (*UKdc*) into next sc (*UKdc*), 7 ch, miss 2 sc (*UKdc*), 1 sc (*UKdc*) into next sc (*UKdc*),* repeat from * to * all around, ending last repeat 5 ch, join with sl st to beg.

Round 4: sl st into first 7 ch loop, into loop work 3 ch, 4 dc (*UKtr*), 4 ch, sl st into 3rd ch from hook (1 picot made), 1 ch, 5 dc (*UKtr*) into loop, *1 sc (*UKdc*) into next 5 ch loop, [5 dc (*UKtr*), 4 ch, sl st into 3rd ch from hook (1 picot made), 5 dc (*UKtr*)] all into next 7 ch loop,* repeat from * to * all around, join with a sl st to beg. Fasten off.

To make up

Place the two snowflakes back to back and sew them together neatly, matching the points as you do so. Sew the large snowflake button to the centre of the snowflake and then sew a small pearl to the centre of each point, using the photograph as a guide.

Thread the ribbon through the top of one point to make a hanging loop. Decide how long you want the ribbon loop to be and trim the ribbon as necessary. Either tie the ends of the ribbon together in a knot or stitch them to form a loop.

Tip

You can spray starch on to the snowflake before attaching the button and beads to give it a firmer texture.

Christmas Stocking

Materials and equipment:

Crochet hook size 2.00mm (US B-1, UK 14)

No. 3 crochet cotton – 1 ball of red and a small amount of white

4 snowflake buttons (8 if you wish to embellish both sides)

Silver ribbon bow

20in (0.5m) of narrow silver ribbon

Sewing needle and thread to match the buttons and ribbon

Measurements:

The Christmas stocking is approximately 4in (10cm) high.

Instructions:

Using white crochet cotton, make 29 ch.

Row 1: 1 sc (*UKdc*) into 2nd ch from hook, 1 sc (*UKdc*) into each ch to end; turn [28 sts].

Rows 2–3: work 1 sc (*UKdc*) into each sc (*UKdc*) to end.

Row 4: join in red. *Insert hook into first sc (*UKdc*) and pull yarn through, then insert hook into corresponding sc (*UKdc*) 2 rows below, draw up loop and work as normal sc (*UKdc*),* repeat to end.

Row 5: using red, work 1 row in sc (*UKdc*).

Row 6: using white, work 1 row in sc (*UKdc*).

Row 7: using white, repeat row 4.

Row 8: using white, work 1 row in sc (*UKdc*).

Rows 9–20: using red, work each st in sc (*UKdc*).

Now create the top of the foot:

Row 1: work in sc (*UKdc*) across 18 sts, turn.

Row 2: work in sc (*UKdc*) across 8 sts, turn.

Rows 3–10: work in sc (*UKdc*) on these 8 sts. Break yarn.

Work foot as follows:

Rejoin yarn and work 10 sc (*UKdc*) along the right side of the top of the foot, 8 sc (*UKdc*) across the toe, and 10 sc (*UKdc*) down the left side of top of the foot then finally work across the remaining 10 sc (*UKdc*) of the foot [48 sts], turn.

Rows 1–6: work in sc (*UKdc*) across all sts.

Row 7: sc (*UKdc*) 2 tog, sc (*UKdc*) 20, sc (*UKdc*) 2 tog twice, sc (*UKdc*) 20, sc (*UKdc*) 2 tog.

Row 8: sc (*UKdc*) 2 tog, sc (*UKdc*) 18, sc (*UKdc*) 2 tog twice, sc (*UKdc*) 18, sc (*UKdc*) 2 tog.

Row 9: sc (*UKdc*) 2 tog, sc (*UKdc*) 16, sc (*UKdc*) 2 tog twice, sc (*UKdc*) 16, sc (*UKdc*) 2 tog.

Row 10: sc (*UKdc*) 2 tog, sc (*UKdc*) 14, sc (*UKdc*) 2 tog twice, sc (*UKdc*) 14, sc (*UKdc*) 2 tog.

Row 11: sc (*UKdc*) 2 tog, work in sc (*UKdc*) to last 2 sts, sc (*UKdc*) 2 tog; fasten off.

To make up
Work in the yarn ends and sew the foot and back seam of the stocking. Attach the snowflake buttons and the ribbon bow, using the photograph as a guide. Fold the silver ribbon in half to make a hanging loop, trimming it to the required length, and attach it to the stocking.

Red–nosed Reindeer

Materials and equipment:

Crochet hook size 2.00mm (US B-1, UK 14)

No. 5 crochet cotton – 1 ball of mid brown and
   1 ball of dark brown

Oddment of red metallic yarn

Black embroidery floss or oddment of black
   crochet cotton

Tiny gold bow and bell embellishment

Small amount of stuffing

Sewing needle and threads to match the yarns

Measurements:

The reindeer is approximately 4in (10cm)
high to the top of his head.

Instructions:

Body

Using mid brown crochet cotton, make 2 sc (UKdc).

Round 1: work 6 sc (UKdc) into 2nd ch from hook then join with a sl st to form a tight circle.

Round 2: work 2 sc (UKdc) into each st around [12 sts].

Round 3: *1 sc (UKdc) into next sc (UKdc), 2 sc (UKdc) into next sc (UKdc),* repeat from * to * all around [18 sts].

Round 4: *1 sc (UKdc) into each of next 2 sc (UKdc), 2 sc (UKdc) into next sc (UKdc),* repeat from * to * all around [24 sts].

Round 5: *1 sc (UKdc) into each of next 3 sc (UKdc), 2 sc (UKdc) into next sc (UKdc),* repeat from * to * all around [30 sts].

Rounds 6–16: work in sc (UKdc) all around.
You will now begin decreasing. Stuff the body as you work.

Round 17: *1 sc (UKdc) into each of next 3 sc (UKdc), sc (UKdc) 2 tog,* repeat from * to * all around.

Round 18: *1 sc (UKdc) into each of next 2 sc (UKdc), sc (UKdc) 2 tog,* repeat from * to * all around.

Round 19: work in sc (UKdc) all around.

Round 20: sc (UKdc) 2 tog all around. Break yarn. Finish stuffing the body and then run the yarn through the last row of sts, draw up and fasten off.

Head

Using mid brown crochet cotton, make 2 sc (UKdc).

Round 1: work 6 sc (UKdc) into 2nd ch from hook then join with a sl st to form a tight circle.

Round 2: work 2 sc (UKdc) into each st around [12 sts].

Round 3: *1 sc (UKdc) into next sc (UKdc), 2 sc (UKdc) into next sc (UKdc),* repeat from * to * all around [18 sts].

Rounds 4–7: work in sc (UKdc) all around.

Round 8: *1 sc (UKdc) into each of next 2 sc (UKdc), 2 sc (UKdc) into next sc (UKdc),* repeat from * to * all around then join with a sl st.

Round 9: work in sc (UKdc) all around then join with a sl st.

Round 10: *1 sc (UKdc) into next sc (UKdc), 2 sc (UKdc) into next sc (UKdc),* repeat from * to * all around then join with a sl st as before.

Rounds 11–15: work 1 sc (UKdc) into each sc (UKdc) all around then join with a sl st as before.
You will now begin decreasing. Stuff the head as you work.

Round 16: *1 sc (UKdc) in each of next 2 sc (UKdc), sc (UKdc) 2 tog,* repeat from * to * all around then join with a sl st as before.

Round 17: work in sc (UKdc) all around then join with a sl st.

Round 18: *1 sc (UKdc) into next sc (UKdc), sc (UKdc) 2 tog,* repeat from * to * all around then join with a sl st.

Round 19: work in sc (UKdc) all around then join with a sl st.

Round 20: sc (UKdc) 2 tog all around then join with a sl st. Fasten off.
Finish stuffing the head, if needed, then run the yarn through the last row of sts and draw up tight. Fasten off.

Front legs (make two)

Using mid brown crochet cotton, make 6 ch.
Row 1: 1 sc (*UKdc*) into 2nd ch from hook, 1 sc (*UKdc*) into each ch to end, turn.
Rows 2–3: work in sc (*UKdc*), increasing 1 sc (*UKdc*) at each end of row.
Work 4 rows in sc (*UKdc*).
Break mid brown and join in dark brown.
Work 2 rows in sc (*UKdc*).
Next row: work in sc (*UKdc*), increasing 1 sc (*UKdc*) at each end of row.
Next row: work in sc (*UKdc*). Fasten off.

Back legs (make two)

Using mid brown crochet cotton, make 10 ch.
Row 1: 1 sc (*UKdc*) into 2nd ch from hook, 1 sc (*UKdc*) into each ch to end, turn.
Row 2: 1 ch, 1 sc (*UKdc*) into each sc (*UKdc*) to end, turn.
Rows 3–4: work in sc (*UKdc*), increasing 1 sc (*UKdc*) at each end of row.
Work 8 rows in sc (*UKdc*).
Change to dark brown and work 4 rows in sc (*UKdc*).
Next row: work in sc (*UKdc*), decreasing 1 sc (*UKdc*) at each end of row.
Next row: repeat previous row. Fasten off.

Large antlers (make two)

Using dark brown crochet cotton, make 12 ch.
Row 1: 1 sc (*UKdc*) into 2nd ch from hook, 1 sc (*UKdc*) into each ch to end, turn.
Rows 2–4: 1 ch, 1 sc (*UKdc*) into each sc (*UKdc*) to end, turn. Fasten off.

Small antlers (make two)

Using dark brown crochet cotton, make 6 ch.
Row 1: 1 sc (*UKdc*) into 2nd ch from hook, 1 sc (*UKdc*) into each ch to end, turn.
Rows 2–4: 1 ch, 1 sc (*UKdc*) into each sc (*UKdc*) to end, turn. Fasten off.

Ears (make two)

Using mid brown crochet cotton, make 2 ch.
Row 1: work 1 sc (*UKdc*) into 2nd ch from hook.
Row 2: 1 ch, 3 sc (*UKdc*) into next sc (*UKdc*), turn.
Rows 3–4: 1 ch, 1 sc (*UKdc*) into each sc (*UKdc*) to end, turn.
Row 5: 1 ch, sc (*UKdc*) 2 tog, 1 sc (*UKdc*) in last sc (*UKdc*), turn.
Row 6: sc (*UKdc*) 2 tog. Fasten off.

Nose

Using red metallic yarn, make 2 ch. Work 14 dc (*UKtr*) into 2nd ch from hook then join with a sl st to first dc (*UKtr*) worked. Fasten off.

To make up

Work in all the ends. Attach the red nose to the head. With black cotton embroider the eyes with French knots and use straight stitches for the mouth. Sew the ears on to each side of the head, using the photograph as a guide. Fold each antler in half lengthways and stitch along the side seam. Sew a short antler on to each long antler at a slight angle, using the photograph as a guide if needed. Now sew the antlers to the head just above the ears. Sew the head on to the body.

Fold the front legs in half lengthways and sew the side seams. Stuff lightly, adding extra at the hoof (dark brown) end to pad them out a little. Oversew a length of cotton through the centre of the hoof end to create the cloven effect. Make up the back legs in the same way. Attach the legs to the body, remembering that Rudolf is sitting down.

Good Fairy

Materials and equipment:

Crochet hook size 2.00mm (US B-1, UK 14)

No. 3 crochet cotton – 1 ball of pale pink, 1 ball of deep pink and small amounts of blue and red for the features

Small amount of gold metallic yarn

2 gold ribbon bows

2 tiny gold self-adhesive craft stars

20in (0.5m) narrow pink ribbon

Cocktail stick

Small piece of gold cushion piping

Sewing needles and thread to match the yarns

Small amount of stuffing

Craft glue

Measurements:

The fairy is approximately 4in (10cm) tall.

Instructions:

Head

Using pale pink crochet cotton, make 2 ch.

Round 1: work 6 sc (*UKdc*) into 2nd ch from hook then join with a sl st to form a tight circle.

Round 2: work 2 sc (*UKdc*) into eachst around [12 sts].

Round 3: *1 sc (*UKdc*) into next sc (*UKdc*), 2 sc (*UKdc*) into next sc (*UKdc*),* repeat from * to * all around [18 sts].

Round 4: *1 sc (*UKdc*) into each of next 2 sc (*UKdc*), 2 sc (*UKdc*) in next sc (*UKdc*),* repeat from * to * all around [24 sts].

Rounds 5–9: work in sc (*UKdc*) all around.

You will now begin decreasing. Stuff the head before you close it up.

Round 10: *1 sc (*UKdc*) into each of next 2 sc (*UKdc*), sc (*UKdc*) 2 tog,* repeat from * to * all around.

Round 11: work in sc (*UKdc*) all around.

Round 12: *1 sc (*UKdc*) into next sc (*UKdc*), sc (*UKdc*) 2 tog,* repeat from * to * all around.

Round 13: work in sc (*UKdc*) all around.

Round 14: sc (*UKdc*) 2 tog all around then join with a sl st. Fasten off.

Body

Using pale pink crochet cotton, make 2 sc (*UKdc*).

Round 1: work 6 sc (*UKdc*) into 2nd ch from hook then join with a sl st to form a tight circle.

Round 2: 2 sc (*UKdc*) into each st around Round 3: *1 sc (*UKdc*) into next sc (*UKdc*), 2 sc (*UKdc*) into next sc (*UKdc*),* repeat from * to * all around [18 sts].

Round 4: *1 sc (*UKdc*) into each of next 2 sc (*UKdc*), 2 sc (*UKdc*) into next sc (*UKdc*),* repeat from * to * all around [24 sts].

Round 5: *1 sc (*UKdc*) into each of next 3 sc (*UKdc*), 2 sc (*UKdc*) into next sc (*UKdc*),* repeat from * to * all around [30 sts].

Rounds 6–14: work in sc (*UKdc*) all around. Fasten off.

Base

Using pale pink crochet cotton, work as body up to end of round 3.

Dress (worked from neck down)

Using dark pink crochet cotton, make 10 ch then join with sl st into a ring.

Round 1: into the ring work 2 ch, 15 sc (*UKdc*) then join with a sl st [16 sc (*UKdc*)].

Round 2: 2 ch, 1 dc (*UKtr*) into same st, 2 dc (*UKtr*) into each sc (*UKdc*) to end, join with a sl st [32 dc (*UKtr*)].

Round 3: 2 ch, 1 dc (*UKtr*) in same st, 2 dc (*UKtr*) into each of next 5 dc (*UKtr*), 4 ch, miss next 4 ch, 2 dc (*UKtr*) into each of next 12 dc (*UKtr*), 4 ch, miss next 4 ch, 2 dc (*UKtr*) into remaining 6 dc (*UKtr*), join with a sl st.

Round 4: *3 ch, miss 1 dc (*UKtr*), sc (*UKdc*) into next dc (*UKtr*) or st,* repeat from * to * all around, do not join.

Round 5: *3 ch, 1 sc (*UKdc*) into 3 ch loop of previous round,* repeat from * to * all around.

Continue as last row until you have eight 3 ch loop rows in all.

Next round: *3 dc (*UKtr*), 3 ch, 3 dc (*UKtr*) into next 3 ch loop, 1 sc (*UKdc*) into next 3 ch loop,* repeat from * to * all around, ending with 3 dc (*UKtr*), 3 ch, 3 dc (*UKtr*), sl st to beg of round.

Next round: join in gold yarn and work 1 sc (*UKdc*) into each st around the base of the skirt.

Arms (make two)

Using pale pink crochet cotton, make 10 ch.

Row 1: 1 sc (*UKdc*) into 2nd ch from hook, 1 sc (*UKdc*) into each ch to end, turn.

Rows 2–4: 1 ch, 1 sc (*UKdc*) into each sc (*UKdc*) to end, turn. Fasten off.

Wings (make two)

Using deep pink crochet cotton, make 2 ch.

Row 1: work 5 dc (*UKtr*) into 2nd ch from hook, turn.

Row 2: 3 ch, 1 dc (*UKtr*) into first st, 2 dc (*UKtr*) into each st to end, turn.

Row 3: join in gold yarn and work 1 sc (*UKdc*) into each st to end, turn.

Row 4: work 2 sc (*UKdc*) into each sc (*UKdc*) to end. Fasten off.

Wand

Take the cocktail stick and wind gold yarn tightly around it. Secure the ends with some craft glue. Stick the two craft stars together with the cocktail stick sandwiched in between them.

To make up

Sew in any loose ends on all pieces. Stuff the body and attach the base. Invert the base a little to enable the fairy to stand up. Place the body inside the dress, thread ribbon through the waist of the dress and tie it firmly to hold the body inside, adding a few stitches if needed; trim the ends. Sew the gold ribbon bow on to the front of the dress.

Fold each arm in half lengthways and stitch the sides. Position an arm on each side of the fairy, pushing it through the armhole of the dress. Sew these in place. Place the wand into one hand and glue in place. Sew the wings together in the centre and stitch these to the back of the fairy.

Unwind the strands of the gold cushion piping using a needle to tease the strands out into ringlets. Cut the strands into equal lengths and glue them to the top of the fairy's head; trim them to a nice shape. Sew a tiny gold bow to the top of the head. Embroider the features. Finally, attach the head to the body.

Baby Penguin

Materials and equipment:

Crochet hook size 2.00mm
  (US B-1, UK 14)
No. 3 crochet cotton – 1 ball of white and 1 ball
  of black
Small amounts of yellow, blue and silver
  metallic yarn
Sewing needle and threads to match the yarn
Small amount of stuffing

Measurements:

The penguin is approximately 3in (8.5cm)
tall, including his hat.

Instructions:

Using white crochet cotton, make 2 ch, work 6 sc (*UKdc*) into 2nd ch from hook then join with sl st into a ring.
Round 1: work 2 sc (*UKdc*) into each sc (*UKdc*) to end then join with a sl st.
Round 2: *1 sc (*UKdc*) into next sc (*UKdc*), 2 sc (*UKdc*) into next sc (*UKdc*),* repeat from * to * all around then join with a sl st as before.
Round 3: *1 sc (*UKdc*) into each of next 2 sc (*UKdc*), 2 sc (*UKdc*) into next sc (*UKdc*),* repeat from * to * all around then join with a sl st as before.
Round 4: *1 sc (*UKdc*) into each of next 3 sc (*UKdc*), 2 sc (*UKdc*) into next sc (*UKdc*),* repeat from * to * all around then join with a sl st as before.
Round 5: 1 sc (*UKdc*) into each of next 4 sc (*UKdc*), 2 sc (*UKdc*) into next sc (*UKdc*),* repeat from * to * all around then join with a sl st as before.

Work 4 rounds in sc (*UKdc*) with no increase.
Change to black and work 4 rounds of sc (*UKdc*).
Now shape the top, stuffing the penguin as you go.
Next round: *1 sc (*UKdc*) into each of next 4 sc (*UKdc*), sc (*UKdc*) 2 tog,* repeat from * to * all around then join with a sl st as before.
Next round: *1 sc (*UKdc*) into each of next 3 sc (*UKdc*), sc (*UKdc*) 2 tog,* repeat from * to * all around then join with a sl st as before.
Next round: *1 sc (*UKdc*) into each of next 2 sc (*UKdc*), sc (*UKdc*) 2 tog,* repeat from * to * all around then join with a sl st as before.
Next round: *1 sc (*UKdc*) into next sc (*UKdc*), sc (*UKdc*) 2 tog,* repeat from

* to * all around then join with a sl st as before.
Next round: sc (*UKdc*) 2 tog all around. Fasten off and run thread through the last row of sts; draw up and fasten off.

Feet (make two)
Using yellow, make 7 ch.
Row 1: 1 sc (*UKdc*) into 2nd ch from hook, 1 sc (*UKdc*) into each ch to end, turn [6 sts].
Row 2: 1 ch, work 1 sc (*UKdc*) into each sc (*UKdc*) to end, turn.
Rows 3–4: work in sc (*UKdc*), decreasing 1 sc (*UKdc*) at each end of row.
Rows 5–6: work in sc (*UKdc*) on these 2 sts.
Rows 7–8: work in sc (*UKdc*), increasing 1 sc (*UKdc*) at each end of row.
Work 2 rows in sc (*UKdc*) on these 6 sts then fasten off.

Beak

Using yellow, make 7 ch.

Row 1: 1 sc (*UKdc*) into 2nd ch from hook, 1 sc (*UKdc*) into each ch to end, turn [6 sts].

Rows 2–3: work in sc (*UKdc*), decreasing 1 sc (*UKdc*) at each end of row.

Rows 4–5: work in sc (*UKdc*) on these 2 sts.

Rows 6–7: work in sc (*UKdc*), increasing 1 sc (*UKdc*) at each end of row.

Work 1 row in sc (*UKdc*) on these 6 sts then fasten off.

Wings (make two)

Using black, make 2 ch.

Row 1: 2 sc (*UKdc*) into 2nd ch from hook, turn.

Row 2: 2 sc (*UKdc*) into first sc (*UKdc*), 1 sc (*UKdc*) into next sc (*UKdc*), turn.

Row 3: 2 sc (*UKdc*) into first sc (*UKdc*), 1 sc (*UKdc*) into next sc (*UKdc*), 2 sc (*UKdc*) into last sc (*UKdc*).

Rows 4–7: work sc (*UKdc*) on these 5 sts.

Rows 8–9: work in sc (*UKdc*), decreasing 1 sc (*UKdc*) at each end of row. Fasten off.

Eyes (make two)

Using white, make 2 ch, work 6 sc (*UKdc*) into 2nd ch from hook then join with a sl st into a ring.

Round 1: 1 ch, work 2 sc (*UKdc*) into each sc (*UKdc*) all around, join with a sl st.

Round 2: 1 ch, *1 sc (*UKdc*) into next sc (*UKdc*), 2 sc (*UKdc*) into next sc (*UKdc*),* repeat from * to * all around, join with a sl st to beg of round. Fasten off.

Pupils (make two)

Using black, make 2 ch. Work 6 sc (*UKdc*) into 2nd ch from hook then join with sl st into a circle.

Hat

Using blue, make 21 ch loosely.

Row 1: work 1 dc (*UKtr*) into 3rd ch from hook, 1 dc (*UKtr*) into each ch to end, turn.

Row 2: 3 ch [counts as 1 dc (*UKtr*)], 1 dc (*UKtr*) into each dc (*UKtr*) to end, turn.

Rows 3–5: 3 ch [counts as 1st dc (*UKtr*)], dc (*UKtr*) 2 tog to last st, 1 dc (*UKtr*) in last st. Fasten off.

Join silver metallic yarn to start of hat and work 1 row of sc (*UKdc*) all along the starting ch edge, fasten off.

Hat bobble

Using silver metallic yarn, make 3 ch. Work 12 dc (*UKtr*) into 3rd ch from hook, join with a sl st. Fasten off. Run thread through row of dc (*UKtr*) and draw up tightly into a little ball. Fasten off.

To make up

Work in all ends. Fold each foot in half and sew up the sides – the wide end is the front of the foot. Sew the feet to the base of the body, angling them outwards slightly. Sew a pupil to each eye then work a French knot in white in the centre of each eye. Place the eyes on the body, using the photograph as a guide, and sew in place. Fold the beak in half and sew the sides. Add a little stuffing to pad slightly. Sew the wide end of the beak to the head. Sew a wing to each side of the body. Sew the side seam of the hat and turn back a brim. Sew the bobble to the top. Pop a little stuffing in the hat then stitch it on to the penguin's head.

Cool Snowman

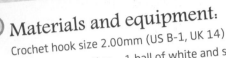

Instructions:

Head

Using white crochet cotton, make 2 ch.

Round 1: work 6 sc (*UKdc*) into 2nd ch from hook then join with a sl st to form a tight circle.

Round 2: work 2 sc (*UKdc*) into each st around then join with a sl st.

Round 3: *1 sc (*UKdc*) into next sc (*UKdc*), 2 sc (*UKdc*) into next sc (*UKdc*),* repeat from * to * all around then join with a sl st as before.

Round 4: *1 sc (*UKdc*) into each of next 2 sc (*UKdc*), 2 sc (*UKdc*) into next sc (*UKdc*),* repeat from * to * all around then join with a sl st.

Rounds 5–9: work in sc (*UKdc*) all around.

You will now begin decreasing. Stuff the head before you close it up.

Round 10: *1 sc (*UKdc*) into each of next 2 sc (*UKdc*), sc (*UKdc*) 2 tog,* repeat from * to * all around then join with a sl st as before.

Round 11: work in sc (*UKdc*) all around.

Round 12: *1 sc (*UKdc*) into next sc (*UKdc*), sc (*UKdc*) 2 tog,* repeat from * to * all around then join with a sl st.

Round 13: work in sc (*UKdc*) all around.

Round 14: sc (*UKdc*) 2 tog all around then join with a sl st.

Fasten off.

Body

Using white crochet cotton, make 2 ch.

Round 1: work 6 sc (*UKdc*) into 2nd ch from hook then join with a sl st to form a tight circle.

Round 2: 2 sc (*UKdc*) into each st around then join with a sl st [12 sts].

Round 3: *1 sc (*UKdc*) into next sc (*UKdc*), 2 sc (*UKdc*) into next sc (*UKdc*),* repeat from * to * all around then join with a sl st.

Round 4: *1 sc (*UKdc*) into each of next 2 sc (*UKdc*), 2 sc (*UKdc*) into next sc (*UKdc*),* repeat from * to * all around then join with a sl st.

Round 5: *1 sc (*UKdc*) into each of next 3 sc (*UKdc*), 2 sc (*UKdc*) into next sc (*UKdc*),* repeat from * to * all around then join with a sl st.

Rounds 6–20 work in sc (*UKdc*) all around. Fasten off.

Base

Using white crochet cotton, make 2 ch.

Round 1: work 6 sc (*UKdc*) into 2nd ch from hook then join with a sl st to form a tight circle.
Round 2: 2 sc (*UKdc*) into each st around then join with a sl st.
Round 3: *1 sc (*UKdc*) into next sc (*UKdc*), 2 sc (*UKdc*) into next sc (*UKdc*),* repeat from * to * all around then join with a sl st.
Round 4: *1 sc (*UKdc*) into each of next 2 sc (*UKdc*), 2 sc (*UKdc*) into next sc (*UKdc*),* repeat from * to * all around then join with a sl st.
Work 1 round in sc (*UKdc*).
Fasten off.

Hat

Using black crochet cotton, make 2 ch.
Round 1: work 6 sc (*UKdc*) into 2nd ch from hook then join with a sl st to form a tight circle.
Round 2: 2 sc (*UKdc*) into each st around then join with a sl st [12 sts].
Round 3: *1 sc (*UKdc*) into next sc (*UKdc*), 2 sc (*UKdc*) into next sc (*UKdc*),* repeat from * to * all around then join with a sl st [18 sts].
Rounds 4–5: work in sc (*UKdc*) all around.
Round 6: work 2 sc (*UKdc*) into each sc (*UKdc*) all around then join with a sl st.
Round 7: work in sc (*UKdc*) all around.
Fasten off.

Scarf

Using green crochet cotton, make 36 ch.
Row 1: work 1 sc (*UKdc*) into 2nd ch from hook, 1 sc (*UKdc*) into each ch to end.
Rows 2–3: work in sc (*UKdc*) to end.
Fasten off.

To make up

Work in all the ends. Stuff the body lightly and then sew the base to the body. Invert the base slightly to make the snowman stand up. Sew the hat on to the head. Embroider the features with black and orange, using the photograph as a guide. Now attach the head to the body. Sew the buttons to the front of the snowman. Wrap mini tinsel around the hat and secure with a stitch. Wrap the scarf around the snowman's neck and secure with a few stitches. Make a hanging loop by crocheting a chain of black cotton, if required, and attach it to the top of the hat.

71

Little Angel

Instructions:

Head

Using pale pink crochet cotton, make 2 ch.

Round 1: work 6 sc (UKdc) into 2nd ch from hook then join with a sl st to form a tight circle.

Round 2: work 2 sc (UKdc) into each st around [12 sts].

Round 3: *1 sc (UKdc) into next sc (UKdc), 2 sc (UKdc) into next sc (UKdc),* repeat from * to * all around [18 sts].

Round 4: *1 sc (UKdc) into each of next 2 sc (UKdc), 2 sc (UKdc) into next sc (UKdc),* repeat from * to * all around [24 sts].

Rounds 5–9: work in sc (UKdc) all around.

You will now begin decreasing. Stuff the head before you close it up.

Round 10: *1 sc (UKdc) into each of next 2 sc (UKdc), sc (UKdc) 2 tog,* repeat from * to * all around.

Round 11: work in sc (UKdc) all around.

Round 12: *1 sc (UKdc) into next sc (UKdc), sc (UKdc) 2 tog,* repeat from * to * all around.

Round 13: work in sc (UKdc) all around.

Round 14: sc (UKdc) 2 tog all around then join with a sl st. Fasten off.

Body

Using white crochet cotton, make 2 sc (UKdc).

Round 1: work 6 sc (UKdc) into 2nd ch from hook then join with a sl st to form a tight circle.

Round 2: 2 sc (UKdc) into each st around [12 sts].

Round 3: *1 sc (UKdc) into next sc (UKdc), 2 sc (UKdc) into next sc (UKdc),* repeat from * to * all around [18 sts].

Round 4: *1 sc (UKdc) into each of next 2 sc (UKdc), 2 sc (UKdc) into next sc (UKdc),* repeat from * to * all around [24 sts].

Round 5: *1 sc (UKdc) into each of next 3 sc (UKdc), 2 sc (UKdc) into next sc (UKdc),* repeat from * to * all around [30 sts].

Rounds 6–14: work in sc (UKdc) all around. Fasten off.

Base

Using white crochet cotton, work as body up to end of round 3.

Dress (worked from neck down)

Using white crochet cotton, make 10 ch then join with a sl st into a ring.

Round 1: into the ring work 2 ch, 15 sc (*UKdc*) then join with a sl st [16 sc (*UKdc*)].

Round 2: 2 ch, 1 dc (*UKtr*) into same st, 2 dc (*UKtr*) into each sc (*UKdc*) to end, join with a sl st [32 dc (*UKtr*)].

Round 3: 2 ch, 1 dc (*UKtr*) in same st, 2 dc (*UKtr*) into each of next 5 dc (*UKtr*), 4 ch, miss next 4 ch, 2 dc (*UKtr*) into each of next 12 dc (*UKtr*), 4 ch, miss next 4 ch, 2 dc (*UKtr*) into remaining 6 dc (*UKtr*), join with a sl st.

Round 4: *3 ch, miss 1 dc (*UKtr*), sc (*UKdc*) into next dc (*UKtr*) or st,* repeat from * to * all around, do not join.

Round 5: *3 ch, 1 sc (*UKdc*) into 3 ch loop of previous round,* repeat from * to * all around.

Round 6: join in silver yarn and work as previous row. Repeat last 2 rows once more. Break silver and continue in white until you have eight 3 ch loop rows in all. Break white and join in silver.

Next round: *3 dc (*UKtr*), 3 ch, 3 dc (*UKtr*) into next 3 ch loop, 1 sc (*UKdc*) into next 3 ch loop,* repeat from * to * all around, ending with 3 dc (*UKtr*), 3 ch, 3 dc (*UKtr*), sl st to beg of round. Fasten off.

Arms (make two)

Using pale pink crochet cotton, make 13 ch.

Row 1: 1 sc (*UKdc*) into 2nd ch from hook, 1 sc (*UKdc*) into each ch to end, turn.

Rows 2–4: 1 ch, 1 sc (*UKdc*) into each sc (*UKdc*) to end, turn. Fasten off.

Halo

Using silver yarn, make 2 ch.

Round 1: work 6 sc (*UKdc*) into 2nd ch from hook then join with sl st into a circle.

Round 2: 1 ch, work 2 sc (*UKdc*) into each sc (*UKdc*) around then join with sl st as before.

Round 3: *3 ch, 1 sc (*UKdc*) into next sc (*UKdc*),* repeat from * to * all around, join as before. Fasten off.

Wings (make two)

Using white crochet cotton, make 2 ch.

Row 1: work 6 dc (*UKtr*) into 2nd ch from hook, turn.

Row 2: 3 ch, 1 dc (*UKtr*) into first st, 2 dc (*UKtr*) into each st to end, turn.

Row 3: repeat row 2.

Row 4: join in silver yarn and work 1 sc (*UKdc*) into each st to end, turn.

Row 5: work 2 sc (*UKdc*) into each sc (*UKdc*) to end. Fasten off.

To make up

Sew in any loose ends on all pieces. Stuff the body and attach the base. Invert the base a little to enable the angel to stand up. Place the body inside the dress, thread ribbon through the waist of the dress and tie it firmly to hold the body inside, adding a few stitches if needed; trim the ends. Sew the silver ribbon bow on to the front of the dress.

Fold each arm in half lengthways and stitch the sides. Position an arm on each side of the angel, pushing it through the armhole of the dress. Sew these in place. Sew the other ends of the arms together, pinching them a little in prayer. Secure with a few stitches. Sew the wings together in the centre then stitch them in place on the back of the angel.

Unwind the strands of the gold cushion piping using a needle to tease the strands out into ringlets. Cut the strands into equal lengths and glue them to the top of the angel's head; trim them to a nice shape. Sew the halo to the back of the head. Embroider the features using black. Finally, attach the head to the body.

73

Christmas Cracker

Materials and equipment:
Crochet hook size 2.00mm (US B-1, UK 14)

No. 5 crochet cotton – 1 ball of green and 1 ball of red

40in (1m) of narrow red satin ribbon

20in (0.5m) of gold ric-rac braid

1 gold rose embellishment

Small piece of card

Small amount of stuffing

Sewing needle and thread to match the yarns

Measurements:
The cracker is approximately 5½in (14cm) long.

Instructions:
Using green crochet cotton, make 27 ch.

Row 1: work 1 dc (*UKtr*) into 3rd ch from hook, 1 dc (*UKtr*) into each ch to end, turn.

Row 2: 1 ch, work 1 sc (*UKdc*) into each dc (*UKtr*) to end, turn.

Row 3: 3 ch, miss first st, work 1 dc (*UKtr*) into each sc (*UKdc*) to end, turn.

Row 4: repeat row 2.

Change to red cotton.

Rows 5–14: repeat rows 3 and 4 five times.

Change to green cotton.

Rows 15–18: repeat rows 3 and 4 twice.

Fasten off.

To make up
Work in the ends. Fold the crochet lengthways to form a tube and then sew the long edges together, matching the colours and rows. The seam will be on the underside of the piece.

Measure a piece of card slightly shorter than the inner red section of the cracker. Roll it into a tube then try the tube inside the crochet to get a good fit. When you are happy with the size, glue the edges of the card together and slip the tube inside the cracker.

Add some stuffing to the inside of the tube to give the cracker more body. Cut the red ribbon into two lengths and tie one tightly to each end of the cracker either side of the tube section, using the photograph as a guide. Trim the ribbon if necessary for a smart finish. Measure a piece of gold ric-rac braid long enough to fit around the central red section and glue it in place with the join on the underside. Glue the gold rose embellishment to the centre as shown in the photograph.

Tip
Hide the join on the ric-rac braid under the rose embellishment for a super-neat finish.

74

Wishing Star

Instructions:

Using white crochet cotton, make 6 ch then join with a sl st into a ring.

Round 1: 1 ch, work 12 sc (*UKdc*) into the ring then join with sl st to first ch.

Round 2: 5 ch, miss 1 sc (*UKdc*), sc (*UKdc*) into next sc (*UKdc*), all around, join to 1st of 5 ch at beg of round [six 5 ch loops].

Round 3: sl st into first 5 ch loop, 2 ch, work 5 dc (*UKtr*) into same loop, 1 sc (*UKdc*) in next sc (*UKdc*). *6 dc (*UKtr*) into 5 ch loop, 1 sc (*UKdc*) into next sc (*UKdc*),* repeat from * to * 4 times more and then join with a sl st to beg of round.

Round 4: sl st to 2nd dc (*UKtr*), 2 ch, 1 dc (*UKtr*) into same dc (*UKtr*), 2 dc (*UKtr*) into each of next 3 dc (*UKtr*), 1 sc (*UKdc*) into next sc (*UKdc*), *miss next dc (*UKtr*), 2 dc (*UKtr*) into each of next 4 dc (*UKtr*), miss 1 dc (*UKtr*), 1 sc (*UKdc*) into sc (*UKdc*),* repeat from * to * 4 times more

and then join with a sl st to beg of round. Break off white.

Round 5: join in metallic yarn to same place as sl st and proceed as follows. Work *1 sc (*UKdc*) into each of the next 4 dc (*UKtr*), **4 ch, sl st into 3rd ch from hook (1 picot formed),** repeat from ** to ** twice more, 1 sc (*UKdc*) into each of the next 4 dc (*UKtr*), 1 sc (*UKdc*) into sc (*UKdc*) of row 4, thus pulling up a long loop,* repeat from * to * 5 times more and then join with a sl st to beg of round. Fasten off.

To make up

Using white thread, stitch the large sparkly button to the centre front of the star. Thread the ribbon through the top of one point to make a hanging loop. Decide how long you want the ribbon loop to be and trim the ribbon as necessary. Either tie the ends of the ribbon together in a knot or stitch them to form a loop.

Christmas Bell

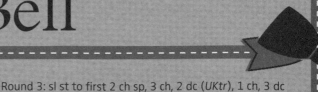

Materials and equipment:

Crochet hook size 2.00mm (US B-1, UK 14)
No. 5 crochet cotton – 1 ball of white
2 burgundy organza ribbon embellishments
20in (0.5m) gold-edged burgundy ribbon
Spray fabric stiffener
Craft glue

Measurements:

The bell is approximately 2¼in (6cm) high,
excluding the ribbon.

Instructions:

Using white crochet cotton, make 8 ch then join with a sl st into a ring.
Round 1: work 16 sc (UKdc) into the ring then join with a sl st.
Round 2: 6 ch, *miss 1 sc (UKdc), 1 dc (UKtr) into next sc (UKdc), 2 ch,* repeat all around, join to 3rd ch of 6 ch at beg of round.

Round 3: sl st to first 2 ch sp, 3 ch, 2 dc (UKtr), 1 ch, 3 dc (UKtr) into same space, *1 sc (UKdc) into next sp, 3 dc (UKtr), 1 ch, 3 dc (UKtr) into next sp,* repeat from * to * twice more, 1 sc (UKdc) into last sp, join to base of first dc (UKtr) of round with a sl st.
Round 4: 5 ch, *4 dc (UKtr), 2 ch, 4 dc (UKtr) into centre of next group, 1 dc (UKtr) into next sc (UKdc),* repeat from * to *, ending last repeat with 1 sl st into 3rd ch of 5 ch at the start of the round.
Round 5: 5 ch, *5 dc (UKtr), 3 ch, 5 dc (UKtr) into centre of next group, 1 dc (UKtr) into next dc (UKtr),* repeat from * to * ending last repeat with 1 sl st into 3rd ch of 5 ch at start of round.
Round 6: 8 ch, 1 sc (UKdc) into centre of next group, *5 ch, 1 dc (UKtr) into next dc (UKtr), 5 ch, 1 sc (UKdc) into centre of next group,* repeat from * to * ending with sl st into 3rd ch of 8 ch made at beg of round.
Round 7: *into next 5 ch sp work [1 sc (UKdc), 1 hdc (UKhtr), 1 dc (UKtr), 1 hdc (UKhtr), 1 sc (UKdc)], 1 sc (UKdc) in next sc (UKdc) or dc (UKtr),* repeat from * to * all around, join with a sl st.
Round 8: * work 1 sc (UKdc) into each sc (UKdc) to dc (UKtr) at point of each group, 3 ch, sl st into base of st just worked (picot made), * repeat from * to * all around, join with a sl st. Fasten off.

Bell clapper
Using white crochet cotton, make 3 ch, work 10 dc (UKtr) into 2nd ch from hook, join with a sl st. Fasten off then run thread through last row, draw up tight into a ball and fasten off. Crochet a chain 2in (5cm) long then fasten off. Attach the ball to the end of the chain firmly.

To make up
Work in all yarn ends on the bell. Spray the bell with starch and then stretch it to shape over a suitable container. Leave it to dry. Pull out the picot points as the starch dries to give a nice shape. When the bell is dry, attach the clapper inside by threading the chain through the hole at the top of the bell and gluing it in place. Make a loop of ribbon and thread it through the top hole in the bell; glue the ends in place. Attach the two organza flowers on either side.

Snowy Fridge Magnet

Materials and equipment:

Crochet hook size 2.00mm (US B-1, UK 14)

No. 5 crochet cotton – 1 ball of white, 1 ball of mid blue and small amounts of black, red, and orange

Silver metallic yarn for the edging

A few small white beads

Small wooden Christmas-tree embellishment, approximately 1½in (4cm) high

Craft glue

Magnetic photo paper

Embroidery needle

Measurements:

The fridge magnet is approximately 3½in (8cm) square.

Instructions:

Background

Using white crochet cotton, make 20 ch.

Row 1: work 1 sc (*UKdc*) into 2nd ch from hook, 1 sc (*UKdc*) into each ch to end, turn.

Row 2: 1 ch, work 1 sc (*UKdc*) into each ch to end, turn.

Rows 3–8: repeat row 2.

Change to mid blue and work 14 rows in sc (*UKdc*). Fasten off.

Join mid blue to any corner of the background crochet. Work 1 round of sc (*UKdc*) all around the piece, working into row ends or stitches; work 3 sc (*UKdc*) into each corner to keep the work flat. Break mid blue and join in silver to work a further round of sc (*UKdc*), treating the corners as before; join to beg with a sl st. Fasten off.

Snowman's head

Using white crochet cotton, make 6 ch then join with a sl st to form a tight ring.

Round 1: work 1 sc (*UKdc*) into each ch to end and then join with a sl st.

Round 2: 1 ch, work 2 sc (*UKdc*) into each sc (*UKdc*) to end and then join as before. Fasten off.

Snowman's body

Using white crochet cotton, make 6 ch then join with a sl st to form a tight ring.

Round 1: work 1 sc (*UKdc*) into each ch to end, join with a sl st.

Round 2: 1 ch, work 2 sc (*UKdc*) into each sc (*UKdc*) to end, join as before.

Round 3: 1 ch, work *1 sc (*UKdc*) into next sc (*UKdc*), 2 sc (*UKdc*) into next sc (*UKdc*),* repeat from * to * all around, join with a sl st.

Snowy Fridge Magnet

Materials and equipment:

Crochet hook size 2.00mm (US B-1, UK 14)

No. 5 crochet cotton – 1 ball of white, 1 ball of mid blue and small amounts of black, red, and orange

Silver metallic yarn for the edging

A few small white beads

Small wooden Christmas-tree embellishment, approximately 1½in (4cm) high

Craft glue

Magnetic photo paper

Embroidery needle

Measurements:

The fridge magnet is approximately 3½in (8cm) square.

Instructions:

Background

Using white crochet cotton, make 20 ch.

Row 1: work 1 sc (*UKdc*) into 2nd ch from hook, 1 sc (*UKdc*) into each ch to end, turn.

Row 2: 1 ch, work 1 sc (*UKdc*) into each ch to end, turn.

Rows 3–8: repeat row 2.

Change to mid blue and work 14 rows in sc (*UKdc*). Fasten off.

Join mid blue to any corner of the background crochet. Work 1 round of sc (*UKdc*) all around the piece, working into row ends or stitches; work 3 sc (*UKdc*) into each corner to keep the work flat. Break mid blue and join in silver to work a further round of sc (*UKdc*), treating the corners as before; join to beg with a sl st. Fasten off.

Snowman's head

Using white crochet cotton, make 6 ch then join with a sl st to form a tight ring.

Round 1: work 1 sc (*UKdc*) into each ch to end and then join with a sl st.

Round 2: 1 ch, work 2 sc (*UKdc*) into each sc (*UKdc*) to end and then join as before. Fasten off.

Snowman's body

Using white crochet cotton, make 6 ch then join with a sl st to form a tight ring.

Round 1: work 1 sc (*UKdc*) into each ch to end, join with a sl st.

Round 2: 1 ch, work 2 sc (*UKdc*) into each sc (*UKdc*) to end, join as before.

Round 3: 1 ch, work *1 sc (*UKdc*) into next sc (*UKdc*), 2 sc (*UKdc*) into next sc (*UKdc*),* repeat from * to * all around, join with a sl st.

Round 4: 1 ch, work *1 sc (*UKdc*) into each of next 2 sc (*UKdc*), 2 sc (*UKdc*) into next sc (*UKdc*),* repeat from * to * all around, join with a sl st. Fasten off.

Snowman's scarf
Using red crochet cotton, make 30 ch and then fasten off.

Snowman's hat
Using black crochet cotton, make 7 ch.
Row 1: 1 ch, work 1 sc (*UKdc*) into each ch to end, turn.
Row 2: *sl st over 2 sc (*UKdc*),* repeat from * to * to last 2 sc (*UKdc*), turn.
Rows 3–4: work each st in sc (*UKdc*). Fasten off.

To make up
Cut a piece of magnetic photo paper the same size as the crocheted background. Using craft glue, stick the paper on to the back of the crocheted background. Press down firmly and allow it to adhere. Sew the snowman's head to his body with a few stitches. Wrap the scarf around his neck and secure. Embroider tiny black dots for eyes and an orange nose. Glue the hat in place on the snowman's head. Stick the snowman on to one side of the background and the tree on to the other, using the photograph as a guide. Glue tiny white beads on to the blue area of the background to suggest falling snow.

Figgy Pudding

Materials and equipment:

Crochet hook size 2.00mm (US B-1, UK 14)

Metallic yarn – 1 ball of brown

No. 3 crochet cotton – small amount of white

20in (0.5m) of white ribbon

Holly berry embellishment

Small amount of stuffing

Craft glue

Measurements:

The figgy pudding is approximately 2¼in (6cm) high.

Instructions:

Using brown metallic yarn, make 2 ch, work 6 sc (*UKdc*) into 2nd ch from hook then join with a sl st into a ring.

Round 1: work 2 sc (*UKdc*) into each sc (*UKdc*) around, join with a sl st.

Round 2: *1 sc (*UKdc*) into next sc (*UKdc*), 2 sc (*UKdc*) into next sc (*UKdc*),* repeat from * to * all around and then join into a circle with a sl st as before.

Round 3: *1 sc (*UKdc*) into each of next 2 sc (*UKdc*), 2 sc (*UKdc*) into next sc (*UKdc*),* repeat from * to * all around and then join with sl st as before.

Round 4: *1 sc (*UKdc*) into each of next 3 sc (*UKdc*), 2 sc (*UKdc*) into next sc (*UKdc*),* repeat from * to * all around and then join with a sl st as before.

Round 5: 1 sc (*UKdc*) into each of next 4 sc (*UKdc*), 2 sc (*UKdc*) into next sc (*UKdc*),* repeat from * to * all around and then join with sl st as before.

Work 8 rounds in sc (*UKdc*) with no increase.

Now you will start the decreases. Stuff the pudding as you go.

Next round: *1 sc (*UKdc*) into each of next 4 sc (*UKdc*), sc (*UKdc*) 2 tog,* repeat from * to * all around and then join with a sl st as before.

Next round: *1 sc (*UKdc*) into each of next 3 sc (*UKdc*), sc (*UKdc*) 2 tog,* repeat from * to * all around and then join with a sl st as before.

Next round: *1 sc (*UKdc*) into each of next 2 sc (*UKdc*), sc (*UKdc*) 2 tog,* repeat from * to * all around and then join with a sl st as before.

Next round: *1 sc (*UKdc*) into next sc (*UKdc*), sc (*UKdc*) 2 tog,* repeat from * to * all around and then join as before.

Next round: sc (*UKdc*) 2 tog all around. Cut the yarn, run the end through the last row of sts, draw up and fasten off.

Iced topping

Using white crochet cotton, make 2 ch. Work 6 sc (*UKdc*) into 2nd ch from hook then join with a sl st into a ring.

Round 1: (RS) work 2 sc (*UKdc*) into each sc (*UKdc*) all around and then join with a sl st.

Round 2: *1 sc (*UKdc*) into next sc (*UKdc*), 2 sc (*UKdc*) into next sc (*UKdc*),* repeat from * to * all around and then join with a sl st as before.

Round 3: *1 sc (*UKdc*) into each of next 2 sc (*UKdc*), 2 sc (*UKdc*) into next sc (*UKdc*),* repeat from * to * all around and then join with a sl st as before.

Round 4: *1 sc (*UKdc*) into each of next 3 sc (*UKdc*), 2 sc (*UKdc*) into next sc (*UKdc*),* repeat from * to * all around and then join with a sl st as before.

Round 5: 1 sc (*UKdc*) into each of next 4 sc (*UKdc*), 2 sc (*UKdc*) into next sc (*UKdc*),* repeat from * to * all around and then join with a sl st as before.

Work 4 rounds in sc (*UKdc*) without further shaping.

Next round: working with the WS facing: *1 dc (*UKtr*) into next sc (*UKdc*), sl st into next sc (*UKdc*),* repeat from * to * all around and then join as before. Fasten off.

To make up

Work in any loose ends neatly. Place the iced topping over one end of the pudding and stitch in place all around. Push the holly embellishment through the centre of the icing and secure it with a few stitches or a little craft glue.

Thread the ribbon through the top of the pudding to make a hanging loop. Decide how long you want the ribbon loop to be and trim the ribbon as necessary. Either tie the ends of the ribbon together in a knot or stitch them to form a loop.

Tabletop Tree

Instructions:

Tree

Using green crochet cotton, make 40 ch and join with a sl st into a circle, being careful not to twist the chain.

Round 1: work 1 sc (*UKdc*) into each ch around then join with a sl st to beg of round [40 sts].

Work a further 3 rounds of sc (*UKdc*).

Round 5: *1 sc (*UKdc*) into each of next 3 sc (*UKdc*), sc (*UKdc*) 2 tog,* repeat from * to * all around [32 sts].

Work 4 rounds in sc (*UKdc*).

Next round: *1 sc (*UKdc*) into each of next 2 sc (*UKdc*), sc (*UKdc*) 2 tog,* repeat from * to * all around [24 sts].

Work 4 rounds in sc (*UKdc*).

Next round: *1 sc (*UKdc*) into next sc (*UKdc*), sc (*UKdc*) 2 tog,* repeat from * to * all around [16 sts].

Work 4 rounds in sc (*UKdc*).

Next round: sc (*UKdc*) 2 tog all around [8 sts].

Work 2 rounds in sc (*UKdc*).

Next round: sc (*UKdc*) 2 tog all around. Fasten off.

Base

Using green, make 2 ch.

Round 1: work 6 sc (*UKdc*) into 2nd ch from hook then join with a sl st into a tight circle.

Round 2: 2 sc (*UKdc*) into each st around then join with a sl st to beg [12 sts].

Round 3: *1 sc (*UKdc*) into next sc (*UKdc*), 2 sc (*UKdc*) into next sc (*UKdc*),* repeat from * to * all around then join with a sl st as before [18 sts].

Round 4: *1 sc (*UKdc*) into each of next 2 sc (*UKdc*), 2 sc (*UKdc*) into next sc (*UKdc*),* repeat from * to * all around then join with a sl st [24 sts].

Round 5: * 1 sc (*UKdc*) into each of next 3 sc (*UKdc*), 2 sc (*UKdc*) into next sc (*UKdc*),* repeat from * to * all around then join with a sl st [30 sts].

Round 6: 1 sc (*UKdc*) into each of next 4 sc (*UKdc*), 2 sc (*UKdc*) into next sc (*UKdc*),* repeat from * to * all around then join with a sl st [36 sts].

Round 7: 1 sc (*UKdc*) into each of next 5 sc (*UKdc*), 2 sc (*UKdc*) into next sc (*UKdc*),* repeat from * to * all around then join with a sl st [42 sts]. Fasten off.

Twisted strands (make one in each of four sizes)
Using variegated green crochet cotton, make 20 ch. Work 1 dc (*UKtr*) into 3rd ch from hook, then 3 dc (*UKtr*) into each ch to end. The crochet will twist as you work. Fasten off. Repeat the process starting with 28 ch, 30 ch and 36 ch.

To make up
Work in all the ends. Stuff the tree quite firmly then attach the base, inverting it slightly to enable the tree to stand. Take each twisted strand and sew the ends together to form a circle. Place the circles on the tree in size order, starting with the largest at the base. Sew in place. Wrap some tinsel around the tree, securing it with a little craft glue or stitches. Glue the tinsel balls on to the branches at random. Cut the cocktail stick in half. Place a little glue on one side of a star and press the other star on to it, sandwiching half the cocktail stick in between. Press firmly until well stuck. Push the cocktail stick down into the top of the tree, securing it with a little glue.

Yuletide Coaster

Instructions:

Using bright red, make 27ch.
Row 1: (RS) work 1 sc (*UKdc*) into 2nd ch from hook, 1 sc
(*UKdc*) into each ch to end, turn [26 sts].
Row 2: 1 ch, *1 sc (*UKdc*) into next sc (*UKdc*), 1 dc (*UKtr*)
into next sc (*UKdc*),* repeat from * to * to end, turn.
Row 3: 1 ch, miss 1 st, *1 dc (*UKtr*) into next sc (*UKdc*), 1
sc (*UKdc*) into next dc (*UKtr*),* repeat from * to * to last st,
1 dc (*UKtr*) into last st, turn.
Rows 2 and 3 form the pattern and are repeated. Work a
further 4 rows in pattern.
Join in variegated green yarn, and work 2 rows
in pattern.
Break green and continue in bright red, working the 2
pattern rows until the piece measures 5in (13cm).
Fasten off.

Edging

Join the variegated green yarn to any corner and work 1
round of sc (*UKdc*) all around, working 3 sc (*UKdc*) into
each corner to keep the work flat.
Next row: turn the work so that the WS is facing and work
*1 dc (*UKtr*) into next sc (*UKdc*), sl st into next sc (*UKdc*),*
repeat from * to * all around then fasten off.

Holly leaf

Using metallic green, make 8 ch, 1 sc (*UKdc*) into 2nd ch
from hook, *1 hdc (*UKhtr*) in next ch, 3 ch, 1 sl st into top
of hdc (*UKhtr*), 1 sc (*UKdc*) into next ch,* repeat from * to
* twice more. Now work in the same way along the other
side of the starting ch; sl st into last ch and then fasten off.
Repeat to make a second leaf using dark green.

Berry

Using dark red, make 3 ch, work 12 dc (*UKtr*) into 2nd ch
from hook then join with a sl st. Break the yarn and run
through top of sts; draw up into a tight ball.

To make up

Work in the ends on all pieces. Press the coaster lightly
using a damp cloth and warm iron to flatten it. Arrange
the holly leaves and berry on the coaster using the
photograph as a guide. Sew them in place.

Festive Napkin Ring

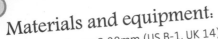

Materials and equipment:

Crochet hook size 2.00mm (US B-1, UK 14)

No. 5 crochet cotton – 1 ball of white

Gold metallic yarn

Needle and white thread

Measurements:

The napkin ring is approximately 3¼in (8cm) wide and 2¼in (6cm) tall and will fit an average napkin.

Instructions:

Napkin ring

Using white crochet cotton, make 16 ch.

Row 1: work 1 sc (UKdc) into 2nd ch from hook, 1 sc (UKdc) into each ch to end, turn.

Rows 2–7 form the pattern. Carry the gold yarn neatly up the side of the work as you proceed, twisting the yarns together to keep them neat.

Rows 2–5: using white, 1 ch, work 1 sc (UKdc) into each sc (UKdc) to end, turn.

Rows 6–7: using gold metallic yarn, repeat row 2.

Work 8 more pattern repeats, then work rows 2–5 one more time. Fasten off.

Join white yarn to one long edge, with the WS facing. Work *1 dc (UKtr), 1 sc (UKdc),* repeat from * to * all along the edge, fasten off. Repeat along the other long edge.

Rose petals

Using white crochet cotton, make 6 ch then join with a sl st into a ring.

Round 1: 1 ch, work 12 sc (UKdc) into the ring, join with a sl st to first ch.

Round 2: *5 ch, miss 1 sc (UKdc), 1 sc (UKdc) into next sc (UKdc),* repeat from * to * all around, join to 1st of 5 ch at beg of round [six 5 ch loops].

Round 3: sl st into first 5 ch loop, 2 ch, work 5 dc (UKtr) into same loop, 1 sc (UKdc) in next sc (UKdc), *6 dc (UKtr) into 5 ch loop, 1 sc (UKdc) into next sc (UKdc),* repeat from * to * 4 times more and then join with a sl st to beg of round.

Round 4: sl st to 2nd dc (UKtr), 2 ch, 1 dc (UKtr) into same dc (UKtr), 2 dc (UKtr) into each of next 3 dc (UKtr), 1 sc (UKdc) into next sc (UKdc), *miss next dc (UKtr), 2 dc (UKtr) into each of next 4 dc (UKtr), miss 1 dc (UKtr), 1 sc (UKdc) into sc (UKdc),* repeat from * to * 4 times more and then join with a sl st to beg of round. Break off yarn.

Round 5: join in gold to same place as sl st and work *1 sc (UKdc) into each of the next 4 dc (UKtr), 3 ch, sl st into 1st of the these ch (1 picot formed), 1 sc (UKdc) into each of the next 4 dc (UKtr), 1 sc (UKdc) into corresponding sc (UKdc) of row 3, thus pulling up a long loop,* repeat from * to * 5 times more, join with a sl st to beg of round. Fasten off.

Rose centre

Using white crochet cotton, make 30 ch.

Row 1: work 1 dc (*UKtr*) into 3rd ch from hook, 3 dc (*UKtr*) into each ch to end.

Break white and join in gold, turn.

Row 2: work 1 sc (*UKdc*) into each dc (*UKtr*) to end.

To make up

Join the shorts ends of the napkin ring neatly and work in all the yarn ends. Work in all ends on the rose pieces. Coil the rose centre tightly and sew in place on the petals. Sew the flower to the napkin ring.

Christmas Bear

Instructions:

Head

Using the 2.00mm (US B-1, UK 14) hook and beige yarn, make 2 ch. Work 6 sc (*UKdc*) into 2nd ch from hook then join with a sl st into a circle.

Round 1: work 2 sc (*UKdc*) into each sc (*UKdc*) around then join with a sl st [12 sts].

Round 2: *1 sc (*UKdc*) into next sc (*UKdc*), 2 sc (*UKdc*) into next sc (*UKdc*),* repeat from * to * all around, join with a sl st as before.

Round 3: *1 sc (*UKdc*) into each of next 2 sc (*UKdc*), 2 sc (*UKdc*) into next sc (*UKdc*),* repeat from * to * all around, join with a sl st as before.

Round 4: *1 sc (*UKdc*) into each of next 3 sc (*UKdc*), 2 sc (*UKdc*) into next sc (*UKdc*),* repeat from * to * all around, join with a sl st as before.

Round 5: 1 sc (*UKdc*) into each of next 4 sc (*UKdc*), 2 sc (*UKdc*) into next sc (*UKdc*),* repeat from * to * all around, join with a sl st as before.

Work 8 rounds in sc (*UKdc*) with no increase.

Now shape the top, stuffing the head as you go.

Next round: *1 sc (*UKdc*) into each of next 4 sc (*UKdc*), sc (*UKdc*) 2 tog,* repeat from * to * all around, join with a sl st as before.

Next round: *1 sc (*UKdc*) into each of next 3 sc (*UKdc*), sc (*UKdc*) 2 tog,* repeat from * to * all around, join with a sl st as before.

Next round: *1 sc (*UKdc*) into each of next 2 sc (*UKdc*), sc (*UKdc*) 2 tog,* repeat from * to * all around, join with a sl st as before.

Next round: *1 sc (*UKdc*) into next sc (*UKdc*), sc (*UKdc*) 2 tog,* repeat from * to * all around, join with a sl st as before.

Next round: sc (*UKdc*) 2 tog all around. Fasten off and run thread through last row of sts; draw up and fasten off.

Muzzle

Using the 2.00mm (US B-1, UK 14) hook and mid brown yarn, make 2 ch. Work 6 sc (*UKdc*) into 2nd ch from hook then join with a sl st into a circle.

Round 1: work 2 sc (*UKdc*) into each

sc (*UKdc*) to end, join with a sl st [12 sts].
Round 2: *1 sc (*UKdc*) into next sc (*UKdc*), 2 sc (*UKdc*) into next sc (*UKdc*),* repeat from * to * all around, join with a sl st as before.
Round 3: *1 sc (*UKdc*) into next 2 sc (*UKdc*), 2 sc (*UKdc*) into next sc (*UKdc*),* repeat from * to * all around, join with a sl st as before. Fasten off.

Ear (make one)
Using the 2.00mm (US B-1, UK 14) hook and mid brown yarn make 2 ch. Work 6 sc (*UKdc*) into 2nd ch from hook then join with a sl st into a circle.
Round 1: work 2 sc (*UKdc*) into each sc (*UKdc*) to end, join with a sl st.
Round 2: work 1 sc (*UKdc*) into each sc (*UKdc*) to end. Fasten off.

Hat
Using the 2.00mm (US B-1, UK 14) hook and red yarn make 32 ch.
Row 1: 1 hdc (*UKhtr*) into 3rd ch from hook, 1 hdc (*UKhtr*) into each ch to end, turn.
Row 2: 1 ch, 1 sc (*UKdc*) into each hdc (*UKhtr*) to end, turn.
Row 3: 2 ch [counts as first hdc (*UKhtr*)], 1 hdc (*UKhtr*) into each sc (*UKdc*) to end.
Row 4: repeat row 2.
Row 5: 2 ch [counts as first hdc (*UKhtr*)], 1 hdc (*UKhtr*) into each of next 2 hdc (*UKhtr*) ,* hdc (*UKhtr*) 2 tog, 1 hdc (*UKhtr*) into each of next 3 hdc (*UKhtr*),* repeat from * to * ending last repeat with hdc (*UKhtr*) 2 tog, hdc (*UKhtr*) into each of last 2 sc (*UKdc*). Turn.
Row 6: 1 ch, 1 sc (*UKdc*) into each sc (*UKdc*) to end.
Row 7: 2 ch [counts as first hdc (*UKhtr*)], *hdc (*UKhtr*) 2 tog, 1 hdc (*UKhtr*) into next sc (*UKdc*),* repeat from * to * ending last repeat with hdc (*UKhtr*) 2 tog, hdc (*UKhtr*) into

each of last 2 sc (*UKdc*). Turn.
Row 8: repeat row 6.
Row 9: 2 ch [counts as first hdc (*UKhtr*)], *hdc (*UKhtr*) 2 tog,* repeat from * to * to last st, hdc (*UKhtr*) into last sc (*UKdc*).
Rows 10–15: work in hdc (*UKhtr*).
Row 16: hdc (*UKhtr*) 2 tog to end of row. Fasten off.
Using the 4.00mm (US G-6, UK 8) hook and eyelash yarn, make a chain long enough to wrap around the brim of the hat twice, fasten off.

Holly leaf (make two)
Using the 2.00mm (US B-1, UK 14) hook and green yarn, make 5 ch. 1 sc (*UKdc*) into 2nd ch from hook, 2 ch, *sl st into top of sc (*UKdc*) just worked, 1 sc (*UKdc*) into next ch, 2 ch, sl st into top of sc (*UKdc*) just worked,* repeat from * to * once more. Fasten off.
Sew the leaves together as a pair. Sew a tiny red bead on to one end of the leaf to depict a berry.

To make up
Sew in any loose ends. Sew the hat seam and attach the bell to the point at the top. Wrap the eyelash chain twice around the brim of the hat to make a fluffy border and stitch it in place. Attach the holly leaf to one side of the hat.

Sew the muzzle on to the front of the head, stuffing it lightly to give it shape. Using dark brown, embroider the nose, mouth, eyes and eyebrows. Sew the ear in position. Only one ear is used because the hat sits on the other side of the head. Sew the hat to the head.

Thread the ribbon through the hat to make a hanging loop. Decide how long you want the ribbon loop to be and trim the ribbon as necessary. Either tie the ends of the ribbon together in a knot or stitch them to form a loop.

Poinsettia Gift Topper

Materials and equipment:
Crochet hook size 2.00mm (US B-1, UK 14)
Metallic yarn – 1 ball each of red, green and gold
35½in (90cm) of red gold-edged satin ribbon,
    1in (2.5cm) wide
Gold flower bead stamens
Fine florist's wire or rose wire
Sewing needle and red thread

Measurements:
Each flower is approximately 2¼in (6cm)
in diameter.

Instructions:

Flower 1 (six petals)
Using red yarn, make 6 ch then join with sl st into a ring.
Round 1: 1 ch, work 12 sc (*UKdc*) into the ring, join with a sl st to first ch.
Round 2: *5 ch, miss 1 sc (*UKdc*), 1 sc (*UKdc*) into next sc (*UKdc*),* repeat from * to * all around, join to 1st of 5 ch at beg of round [six 5 ch loops].

Round 3: sl st into first 5 ch loop, 2 ch, work 5 dc (*UKtr*) into same loop, 1 sc (*UKdc*) in next sc (*UKdc*), *6 dc (*UKtr*) into 5 ch loop, 1 sc (*UKdc*) into next sc (*UKdc*),* repeat from * to * 4 times more, join with a sl st to beg of round.
Round 4: sl st to 2nd dc (*UKtr*), 2 ch, 1 dc (*UKtr*) into same dc (*UKtr*), 2 dc (*UKtr*) into each of next 3 dc (*UKtr*), 1 sc (*UKdc*) into next sc (*UKdc*),* miss next dc (*UKtr*), 2 dc (*UKtr*) into each of next 4 dc (*UKtr*), miss 1 dc (*UKtr*), 1 sc (*UKdc*) into sc (*UKdc*),* repeat from * to * 4 times more and then join with a sl st to beg of round. Break off red.
Round 5: join in gold to same place as sl st and work *1 sc (*UKdc*) into each of the next 4 dc (*UKtr*), 3 ch, sl st into 1st of the these ch (1 picot formed), 1 sc (*UKdc*) into each of the next 4 dc (*UKtr*), 1 sc (*UKdc*) into corresponding sc (*UKdc*) of row 3, thus pulling up a long loop,* repeat from * to * 5 times more, join with a sl st to beg of round. Fasten off.

Flower 2 (eight petals)
Using red yarn, make 8 ch then join with a sl st into a ring.
Round 1: 1 ch, work 16 sc (*UKdc*) into the ring, join with a sl st to first ch.
Round 2: 1 ch, sc (*UKdc*) into same st as join, *1 ch, miss next sc (*UKdc*), sc (*UKdc*) into next ch, 8 ch, sc (*UKdc*) into same st,* repeat from * to * 6 times more, 1 ch, sc (*UKdc*) into same st as the first sc (*UKdc*), 4 ch, tr (*UKdtr*) into first sc (*UKdc*) to join [8 loops made].
Round 3: 3 ch to count as first dc (*UKtr*), work 7 more dc (*UKtr*) into the same loop (around the post of the dc (*UKtr*) in round 2), 1 sc (*UKdc*) into the next 1 ch sp, *15 dc (*UKtr*) into the next 8 ch loop, 1 sc (*UKdc*) in the next 1ch sp,* repeat from * to * 6 times more, 7 dc (*UKtr*) into the first loop, join with a sl st to the top of beg 3 ch [8 petals made]. Break off red.
Round 4: join in gold with a sl st to beg of previous round, work 1 sc (*UKdc*) into each sc (*UKdc*) all around each petal, join with a sl st to beg of round. Fasten off.

Leaves (make three)
Using green yarn, make 13 ch.
Work 1 sc (*UKdc*) into 2nd ch from hook, 1 hdc (*UKhtr*)

into each of next 2 ch, 1 dc (*UKtr*) into each of next 2 ch, 1 tr (*UKdtr*) into each of next 2 ch, 1 dc (*UKtr*) into each of next 2 ch, 1 hdc (*UKhtr*) into next 2 ch, 1 sc (*UKdc*) into last ch. Make 1 ch, now work along the other side of the foundation in the same way, join with a sl st.

To make up
Work in the ends neatly on all the pieces. Take a wire stamen and spread the beads into a flat shape. Insert it through the centre of a flower, twist the wire into a neat coil at the back of the flower and secure with some firm stitches using a needle and red thread. Repeat with the other flower.

To make a bow
Cut the red ribbon into three 12in (30cm) lengths. Find the points 3in (7.5cm) from each end of the first length. Pinch the ribbon at these points and bring the pinches together. Squash the ribbon loop between the pinched folds so it is flat and centred at the folds. Repeat with the other ribbon lengths. When you are satisfied with the result, assemble the bows then take some fine wire and twist it tightly around the centre. Arrange the loops and tails of the ribbon in a pleasing manner then trim the tails if desired. Arrange the flowers and leaves on to the centre of the ribbon, pin in position and then sew in place.

Knitting projects

Twinkling Star
page 10

Christmas Tree
page 12

Gingerbread Heart
page 14

Tiny Sweater
page 16

Mini Mittens
page 18

Christmas Mouse
page 20

Fairy Mouse
page 22

Stocking
page 24

Holly Garland
page 26

Sweetie Cone
page 28

Fir Tree Egg Cosy
page 30

Rudolph
page 32

Jolly Snowman
page 34

Rocking Robin
page 36

Christmas Pud
page 38

Christmas Angel
page 40

What a Hoot
page 42

French Hen
page 44

Turtle Dove
page 46

Nordic Bunting
page 48

Crochet projects

Pine Cone
page 54

Festive Wreath
Page 56

Dove or Peace
page 58

Glimmering Snowflake
page 60

Christmas Stocking
page 62

Red-nosed Reindeer
page 64

Good Fairy
page 66

Baby Penguin
page 68

Cool Snowman
page 70

Little Angel
page 72

Christmas Cracker
page 74

Wishing Star
page 76

Christmas Bell
page 78

Snowy Fridge Magnet
page 80

Figgy Pudding
page 82

Tabletop Tree
page 84

Yuletide Coaster
page 86

Festive Napkin Ring
puge 88

Christmas Bear
page 90

Poinsettia Gift Topper
page 92

95

Publisher's Note
If you would like more information about
knitting and crochet, try the following books
by Search Press:
Beginner's Guide to Knitting by Alison Dupernex,
Search Press, 2004
Beginner's Guide to Crochet by Pauline Turner,
Search Press, 2005.

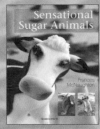